$\mathcal{A}$MA$\approx$ING
O·H·I·O

$\mathcal{A}$MA≈ING
O·H·I·O

By Damaine Vonada

ORANGE FRAZER PRESS • WILMINGTON, OHIO

Library of Congress Catalog
Card Number: 89-091611

ISBN 0-9619637-3-5

Published by
Orange Frazer Press, Inc.
Main Street, Box 214
Wilmington, Ohio 45177

ACKNOWLEDGEMENTS

Special thanks to Marcy Hawley, Wilmington, Ohio, for her generous contributions to the Origins chapter; the editorial staff and management of Orange Frazer Press, Inc., for their continued interest and support; and, for their invaluable research assistance, the following individuals and institutions: Gertrude Jacob, Volunteer in Research, Oberlin College Archives; Mary Ellen Sears, Public Relations, Ohio Bell, Dayton; Ohio Bell Library, Cleveland; Ken Bartter, General Telephone of Ohio; Hayner Cultural Center, Troy, Ohio; Clay Herrick, Cleveland Landmarks Commission; Bonnie K. Kopen, Public Relations, Huntington National Bank, Cleveland; Linda S. Ellis, Public Affairs, NASA Lewis Research Center, Cleveland; Rick Ewig, Wyoming State Archives, Museums, & Historical Department, Cheyenne, Wyoming; Anita Gundlach Feick, Sandusky, Ohio; the librarians of the Greene County District Library and branches; and, especially, to the librarians and skilled Reference Staff of Adult Services, The Dayton and Montgomery County Public Library.

Research assistance: Dave Stephenson, Columbus

Design: Brooke Wenstrup, Columbus

Illustrations: A. Brian Zampier, SM, Dayton

Typography: Hans Seiler, Washington C.H.

Cover: Corson Hirschfeld, Cincinnati

CONTENTS

■

FOREWORD

"Some are born great.
Some achieve greatness.
And some are born in Ohio."
— *James Ford Rhodes*

Henry Howe, the erstwhile historian of the 1800's, spent both his youth and old age in Ohio. His travels across the state yielded four fat volumes, which quite adequately supported his observation that "Ohio proved a mine of ungathered history; all one had to do was travel and pick it up." Ohio is still a prodigious mine of history, but we presumed to spare these folks from going to Mr. Howe's considerable trouble. This armchair journey is not about history, or even geography, *per se*. Instead, we offer a perspective: Ohio and two centuries of its citizenry seen in various facets — from our Founders to their Feuds and Foibles. We want to inform the reader about ironic and anecdotal aspects of Ohio; to introduce him to events, institutions, and people he does not know; and to deepen his acquaintance with those he does. Frankly, we hope that the reader will find the folks whom he meets on these pages amazing. We chose them because they had a national and even international influence. Their lives, livelihoods, obsessions, duties, decisions, and passions helped shape, and in some cases, define our nation. Given their far-reaching and long-lasting affect, we think the reader will be persuaded that novelist Herman Melville pegged them perfectly: "a right sturdy set of fellows . . . ever seeking to push their brethren to the uttermost."

Damaine Vonada

Dayton, Ohio
June, 1989

"Genius is one per-cent inspiration and ninety-nine percent perspiration."
— *Edison*

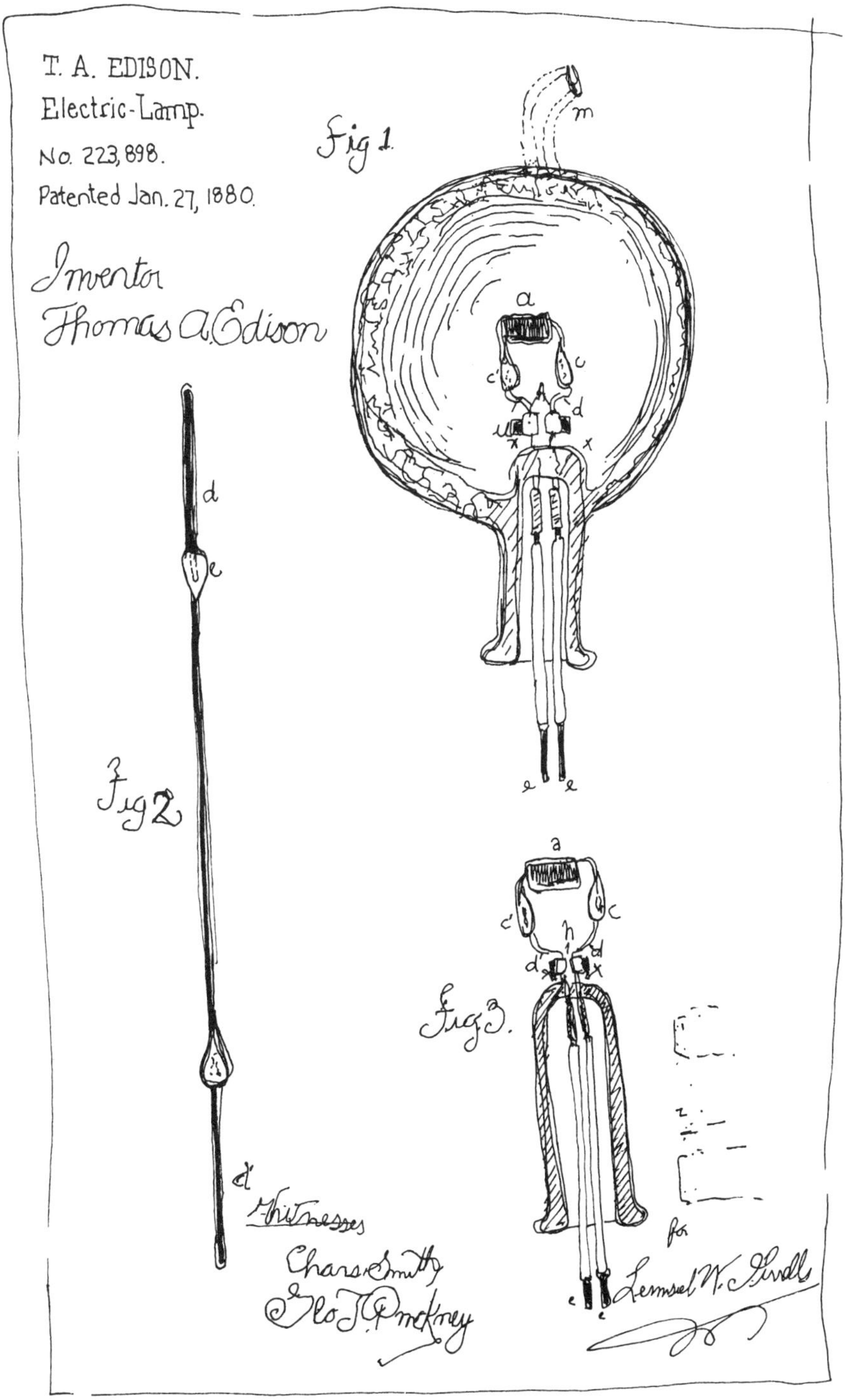

T. A. EDISON.
Electric-Lamp.
No. 223,898.
Patented Jan. 27, 1880.

Fig 1.

Inventor
Thomas A. Edison

Fig 2

Fig 3.

Witnesses
Chas. Smith
Geo. T. Pinckney

Lemuel W. Serrell

■ THE LONG ARM OF OHIO

■ *Concerning cultural and engineering landmarks by native sons and daughters, whose reach has extended sufficiently past the state line to alter the face of America*

▶ In 1886, the capitol of Wyoming consisted of two rented rooms in Cheyenne. In 1888, Wyoming boasted a grand new Neo-Corinthian building in which to conduct affairs of state. This quick change in the state of affairs was caused by the Sandusky firm of A. Feick and Brother, which was the low bidder ($131,275.13) on a contract to build Wyoming's capitol.

It would not be wholly accurate, however, to say that the Feicks — Adam, brother George, and Adam's son, John — merely built a building, for in truth, they imported it, and largely from their home state. What Wyoming, which then was not even yet part of the Union, lacked in construction materials, the Feicks made up for in Ohio. The skilled laborers and millwork came from Sandusky, the interior cherry wood from Buckeye forests, the window glass — and even the architect — from Toledo. In essence, the State Capitol of Wyoming was designed and fabricated in Ohio, then shipped piece by piece to Cheyenne on railroad cars across a thousand miles of prairie.

The Feicks left a landmark where only wide open space had been before, a remarkable enough achievement, but not at all uncommon among Ohioans, whose creative reach often exceeds the grasp of time and imagination, not to mention the state line. In fact, Ohioans have had a hand in preserving, protecting, defending, and certainly making, any number of the cornerstones and touchstones by which our society navigates. Landmarks are something of an Ohio cottage industry for folks like the Feicks, to whom Wyomingites shall always be grateful, not only for bringing the capitol project in under budget but also for delivering the legislature from a long-term lease on those rented rooms.

"You don't see as many drunkards in Cheyenne as you do in Sandusky . . ."
— John A. Feick, writing home from Wyoming, 1887

U.S. Constitution, Bill of Rights, and Declaration of Independence, National Archives, Washington, D.C.
storage vault designed by Mosler Safe Company, Hamilton, 1952

National Christmas Tree, Washington, D.C.
illuminated since 1963 by GE Lighting, Cleveland
transported to its capital site by Davey Tree Expert Company, Kent, 1978

Vietnam Veterans Memorial, Washington, D.C.
designed by Athens's Maya Ying Lin, 1981

Chandeliers in the East Room, the White House
installed by President Ulysses S. Grant

Cherry blossoms, Washington, D.C.
trees brought to U.S. by First Lady Helen Taft of Cincinnati, who persuaded the Japanese to send 3000 cherry trees and personally planted the first ones in the Tidal Basin on March 27, 1912

Supreme Court of the United States, Washington, D.C.
Zanesville native Cass Gilbert, architect, 1935

Woolworth Building, New York City
Cass Gilbert, architect, 1913

Statue of Liberty, New York City
Head and raised arm steps built by J.B. Foote Foundry, Fredericktown, 1987
Brick walkway pavers built by Day-Crume Brick and Block, Dayton, 1987

Statue of George Washington, Federal Hall site, New York City
sculpted by Urbana's John Quincy Adams Ward, 1883

Golden Gate Bridge, San Francisco
designed by Cincinnati's Joseph Strauss, 1937

Electric elevators and steel skeletons made the mighty skyscrapers possible at the turn of the century, but the Woolworth Building in New York City was built on nickels and dimes. Frank Woolworth's chain of stores had raked in so many of them that by 1913, he could literally pay for his $13 million building with pocket change. The nation's large quantity-low price pioneer wanted a monument to his unprecedented business success, and Cass Gilbert's Gothic concept for a skyscraper that soared in height as well as spirit was just the sort of "Cathedral of Commerce" that Woolworth had in mind. Certainly Gilbert gave the building enough of the elements that had graced the great medieval cathedrals — flying buttresses, tourelles, pinnacles, and gargoyles. Rising 792 feet above the sidewalks of Broadway, his skyscraper was the highest building in the world, a breathtaking monument to the economic prowess of both a man and a nation that increasingly believed that the business of America was business. No less than President Woodrow Wilson *threw the switch that lit the Woolworth Building for its formal dedication in 1913, the critics declaring Gilbert's design a masterpiece, and the newspapers chiming in that Mr. Woolworth had bought himself "the greatest mountain of steel and stone ever erected by man." It was a mountain of praise, generated in large part, no doubt, because the Woolworth Building truly looked like a skyscraper — proud, dar-*

Cass Gilbert

Panama Canal
Dug with shovels from Marion Steam Shovel Company, Marion, 1914

Gymnasium Floors, 1988 Seoul Olympic Games
Made by Robbins International, Cincinnati

Berlin Botanical Garden's original buckeye tree, Germany
A 180-year-old specimen grown from Ohio seed, early 1800's

State Capitol of Wyoming
designed by Toledo architect David Gibbs built by A. Feick and Brother, Sandusky, 1888

University of Chicago
started in 1891, with monetary gift from Cleveland's John D. Rockefeller, who eventually padded this seat of learning with $35 million

Laura Spelman Rockefeller Memorial Carillon, New York City
a memorial to Rockefeller's wife, the world's largest carillon boasts the biggest tuned bell in Christendom . . . or anywhere else

United Nations, New York City
site purchased with $8.5 million gift from Cleveland native John D. Rockefeller, Jr.

Colonial Williamsburg, Virginia
restoration undertaken and underwritten by John D. Rockefeller, Jr.

U.S. Flag
fifty-star rendition designed by Robert Heft, Napoleon, circa 1959

U.S. Flag on the Moon
the red-white-and-blue planted on lunar gray by Wapakoneta's Neil Armstrong, who performed the first Moon Walk, 1969

ing, timeless, and reaching for the stars. Before long, of course, other skyscrapers eclipsed the Woolworth Building, and its stature shrank in relation to the Goliaths that filled Manhattan and the other metropolises, but Gilbert had fixed the quintessential image of the skyscraper in the American mind. He and Mr. Woolworth created an icon, a building that still feeds the soul in a time when concrete-and-glass boxes increasingly rob the spirit. The lobby of the Woolworth Building, by the way, contains sculptured caricatures of its principal engineers and planners. Mr. Woolworth is there, holding a nickel, and so is Cass Gilbert, whose moustachioed figure is destined to forever peer at a miniature copy of the Woolworth Building.

■ OHIO DISASTERS

▌ *Thirteen terribly unlucky times, in which Ohioans battled awesome mishaps and misfortunes foisted upon them by the equally formidable forces of Mother Nature and human folly*

▶ National class disasters have struck Ohio several times. Disasters almost by definition always *strike,* a most revealing verb, for it tells how helpless folks feel when calamity suddenly confronts them. But whenever disasters have loosened their grip on the wheel of their own fortune, Ohioans have seized the moment during those tragic times and reacted variously to regain control.

When the first cholera epidemics reached Ohio in 1832, the Governor appealed to the Almighty. He declared a day of fasting and prayer, and Columbus folks hoped that gathering in churches would spare them from the plague. Given the contagiousness of the disease, of course, such congregations were quite counterproductive, and the time would have been better spent in simply washing their hands. A few years later, a Cincinnati woman tried running away from cholera. After sewing her money in her skirt, she took off for the country, but cholera caught her anyway. Folks were so anxious to get her diseased body buried that they didn't even bother to take the gold coins out of her hem.

Disasters have also brought out the best in Ohioans, as people rise to even the nastiest occasions. After the 1913 flood washed away most of Dayton, a relief committee asked Lib Hedges, the city's eminently successful madam, for a modest donation. Lib groused about her own losses for a while, then blurted out, "I'll give two thousand dollars and not a d____d cent more."

And during that flood, National Cash Register President John Henry Patterson became his city's savior. In a single morning, he shifted his production line from business machines to boats and turned his factory into a hospital and relief center. Mothers who gave birth in the "maternity ward" gratefully named their babies "Cash."

But fright and flight and floods aside, consider the sterling reaction of Columbus reporter William Cunningham when a prisoner asked him to notify his family that he had survived the Ohio Penitentiary fire:

"What shall I wire?" asked Cunningham.

"You make it up," said the prisoner.

"How about *escaped*?" he asked.

Ah yes, *escaped.* Given the circumstances, can there be a better response whenever disaster strikes?

THE CHOLERA EPIDEMICS
thousands died — international plague
1800's
entire state

Cholera was the scourge of the nineteenth century, a disease that began in India and spread over the world in successive waves of epidemic. The United States might have gotten off lightly, except for the Industrial Revolution. The advent of rapid transportation and mushrooming urban populations only fueled the contagion.

Cholera traveled to Ohio via the Ohio River and Lake Erie, then was carried inland by canal and stagecoach traffic. People did not know that the cholera bacteria thrives in human waste, a near-suicidal ignorance considering that public sanitation was minimal for most of the century. What they did know — and feared — was that the disease spread like wildfire and that death, given the violence of the gastro-intestinal symptoms, came with merciful swiftness.

The worst year for Ohio was 1849, when cholera raged in all states east of the Rocky Mountains. Cholera never discriminated. It took 120 in the village of Eaton and 8000 in the city of Cincinnati. It claimed the innocent — Harriet Beecher Stowe's baby son — as well as the damned — 116 inmates of the Ohio Penitentiary in Columbus. It delayed the fun of the Ohio State Fair and the business of Cincinnati, where city fathers vainly tried to purify the air with sulphur fires on the streetcorners. Stephens Collins Foster wrote to his worried mother that he was quite well in the city, but

Cure for cholera, printed in the Ohio State Journal, *1849:*

"For an adult, take ⅔ teaspoonful of castor oil and 6 drops of camphor in a half a tablespoon of scalded milk, in 6 hours take 9 drops of balsam caper, in 6 hours, 9 more; in 6 hours the oil again. Take 6 drops of camphor in a teaspoonful of water sweetened with loaf sugar every half hour.

for Mrs. Stowe, cholera was the last straw. After her young Samuel died, she left Cincinnati for good.

OHIO PENITENTIARY FIRE
322 killed — deadliest U.S. prison fire
April 21, 1930
Columbus

A warden once compared the hoary Ohio Penitentiary to the Bastille, and its massive stone walls twenty-four feet high did render the place a grim rock of cages that witnessed torture, epidemic, and execution. But the blackest moment came when a fire apparently started by inmates to divert attention from an escape plan got out of control. Most of the dead were prisoners locked in the "living hell" of cell blocks G and H, where "black smoke was choking the breath out of men," and "steel bars turned so red hot that human beings were being boiled alive."

Prison officials later drew fire of their own for not holding fire drills or unlocking imperiled inmates with all due speed, and the National Guard had to maintain order among the bitter survivors. Ironically, the burnt section of the prison had been considered "fireproof," and it might well have been except for the wooden roof, which was inexplicably made doubly deadly by a heavy, and highly flammable, tarpaulin covering.

COLLINWOOD SCHOOL FIRE
172 children, 2 teachers killed
— deadliest U.S. school fire
March 4, 1908
Collinwood

Fire inspectors blamed the blaze on an overheated steam pipe and the death toll on panic. The rush to escape Lakeview Elementary turned into a stampede, and scores of young bodies were found piled against the doors. Of the 300 or so children in attendance, only 80 escaped harm. Most pitiful of all, perhaps, were the nineteen who could not be identified and had to be buried in a common grave.

Lakeview Elementary was built mostly of wood; too many pupils were crowded inside;

"Some fell at the rear entrance and others stumbled over them. I saw my little Helen among them. I tried to pull her out, but the flames drove me back. I had to leave my little child to die."

— Fred Herter, janitor, Lakeview Elementary School

there was only one fire escape; and the narrow hallways not only impeded safe exit but also acted as giant flues. The school's tragedy taught a cruel lesson, and the entire nation paid attention with beefed up school fire laws and safety standards.

EAST OHIO GAS COMPANY EXPLOSION AND FIRE
130 dead, 20 city blocks devastated
October 20, 1944
Cleveland

Since the war effort fairly devoured natural gas, patriotism could justify building a liquification and storage plant in the middle of the blue collar neighborhood. Because such a commercial gas facility had never been built before, the plant was something of an experiment, and the people living between East 55th and 67th streets became unwitting guinea pigs in a catastrophe. The storage tanks developed cracks, and leaking gas spread a surreptitious carpet of death throughout the neighborhood. As the gas invaded basements and sewers, houses suddenly began exploding. The subsequent fire storm did not even spare the birds. The intense heat reached high into the sky and scorched them out of the air.

CLEVELAND CLINIC FIRE
123 killed — deadliest U.S. hospital fire
May 15, 1929
Cleveland

Overheated x-ray film touched off explosions that sent staff and patients jumping for their lives from the windows and roof. The burning film released nitrogen dioxide, a gas which causes severe lung edema, and deadly yellow clouds rolled through the clinic. The noxious fumes repelled fireman at the doors and forced them to enter the building through a skylight. A physician exposed to the gas died a few hours later; others lingered for days. Every automobile in the city was commandeered to transport victims, and an SOS went out to thirty cities for oxygen tents. In the aftermath, Cleveland firemen got gas masks, and the nation got new ways of handling and storing hazardous

Consumed in the East Ohio Gas Company Explosion:
217 automobiles
79 houses
8 stores
7 trailers
2 factories
1 tractor
Estimated property damage: $6 million

Pacific Express No. 5 — two engines, 11 cars, and 159 passengers and crew — was crossing the bridge with snail-pace caution about seven-thirty p.m. The engineer in Socrates, *the lead locomotive, heard a loud crack. He looked over his shoulder to see the locomotive* Columbia *and its long trail of cars dropping away toward the gorge. Immediately, the engineer opened throttle and managed to get* Socrates *safely to a bridge abuttment, where he blasted the whistle again and again to summon help. The* Columbia, *meanwhile, had turned upside down on top of an express car and in tandem they plummeted earthward. One by one, the cars toppled, slamming into each other and the rocky gorge. The train's shattered oil lamps and overturned coal stoves touched off fires, and passengers lucky enough to land in the shallow waters of Ashtabula Creek had the best chance to survive. Rescuers later collected five bushels of the passenger's shoes, most of which still contained pieces of foot and bone.*

materials, in particular nitrocellulose x-ray film.

ASHTABULA BRIDGE COLLAPSE
92 killed — deadliest Ohio rail accident
December 29, 1876
Ashtabula

The bridge spanned a deep gorge just east of town, and it fell on a bitter night when the snow was coming down fast and the ill-fated Pacific Express No. 5 was running late. The double track wooden bridge had been built by the Lake Shore and Southern Railroad. Amasa Stone, the railroad president, held the patent on the bridge's iron Howe trusses and was largely responsible for its design. Though experts later concluded that the heavy snow caused a derailment that in turn placed ruinous stress on the bridge, Mr. Stone never escaped personal blame for one of the worst accidents in the history of U.S. railroads.

The breaking point of the bridge, however, proved to be a turning point in bridge engineering. The horror of Ashtabula and the spectacular collapse three years later of Scotland's Tay Bridge offered vivid proof that iron could not support the railroad's ever-increasing loads. Iron was the real culprit at Ashtabula, and the disaster there accelerated the transition to steel bridge construction.

MILLFIELD MINE EXPLOSION
82 killed — deadliest Ohio mine accident
November 5, 1930
Millfield, Athens County

The Sunday Creek Coal Company first learned that there was a problem at Mine No. 6 when a farmer telephoned that he had just seen a man being blown out of the new air shaft. A short circuit touched off a pocket of methane gas shortly before noon. It took four hours of digging through debris before rescuers could bring in the canaries and another three hours before they found the first body. In addition to the burned and suffocated miners, the Sunday Creek president and several other company officers perished. They had been inspecting the air shaft, recently installed in what they thought was the safest mine for miles.

LORAIN TORNADO
85 killed — worst Ohio twister
June 28, 1924
Lorain

A musical was in progress when a tornado took the roof off Sandusky's State Theatre about 5 p.m. The house went dark, and the stunned audience dodged bricks and broken glass, but the pianist gamely kept on playing. After delivering its initial blow to Sandusky, the twister traveled twenty-five miles across Lake Erie and saved the knockout punch for Lorain: 200 stores and 500 houses destroyed, more than 1,000 people injured, and about one-fourth of the town — some 10,000 — homeless. Because Governor Donahey would not seek federal relief funds, the citizens of Lorain rebuilt the town with their own money and donations from fellow Ohioans.

1913 FLOOD
467+ died — worst Ohio flood
March 23-28
Great Miami and Scioto River Valleys

Spring rains and a thaw had already saturated the ground, then an Easter Week cloudburst turned the rivers and their tributaries wild. Though a hundred Ohio cities were inundated, low-lying Dayton (whose founders had ignored the Indians' flood warnings) was hardest hit. Four waterways converge within a mile there, and on March 25, the city was deluged with 1.5 million gallons of water per *second,* an incredible torrent that equalled an entire month's flow over Niagara Falls. River gauges registered a record-setting twenty-nine feet, and fires and explosions added to the toll of dead and injured. But Daytonians pulled themselves up by their own soggy bootstraps, pledging their personal funds as seed money for dams that have not only kept them dry ever since but have also been a national flood protection model.

John Henry Patterson noticed an arm rising out of a swirling eddy of water. Having single-handedly organized the effort to save his entire city, Mr. Patterson now single-mindedly waded into the flood to save one drowning man. Mr. Patterson was short, slight, and elderly; the man was six feet four and weighed more than two hundred pounds. Nonetheless, Mr. Patterson's sheer will got him to the sanctuary of an automobile running board. The fellow turned out to be nineteen year old Ray Stansbury, a foundry worker at Mr. Patterson's cash register factory. The rescue cost the old gentleman his eyeglasses, but it was a justifiable loss, considering that the imperiled Stansbury had exhausted himself that day by carrying nearly two hundred people one-by-one to safety. "Helpfulness," the Dayton Daily News *rightly observed, "was the one occupation . . ."*

THE 1937 FLOOD
250 + dead — major U.S. natural disaster
January, 1937
Ohio River Valley

Someone once wrote that folks along the Ohio River monitor the water level the way that New Yorkers spot gold and Southerners cotton. On January 26, the river watchers got an eyeful as the Ohio crested at a record 79.99 feet, after weeks of unrelenting rain poured an estimated 60 billion tons of water into the valley. The river simply could not hold it all, and the tremendous overflow flooded more than 12,000 square miles of land. From Marietta to the Mississippi River, water closed every bridge, except for Cincinnati's Suspension Bridge, which residents heroically protected with sandbags, even as floating gasoline sparked the city's greatest fire on "Black Sunday." The widespread destruction proved that flood prevention in the Ohio Valley was no longer a local option, and the federal government began to enact the nation's fledgling Flood Control Act.

THE NURSING HOME FIRES
63 and 32 killed — first and second most deadly U.S. nursing home fires
November 22, 1963; January 9, 1970
Fitchville; Marietta

The blazes at Golden Age Nursing Home and Harmar House seemed especially dastardly because they trapped the ill and the infirm, a situation that resulted in nursing homes being required to have automatic sprinkler systems to give residents a fighting chance. So far, so good: Harmar House was Ohio's last multiple fatality nursing home fire.

THE XENIA TORNADO
34 killed — focal point of a national disaster
April 3, 1974
Xenia

When two unusually strong fronts — one warm and moist, one cold and dry — collided over the Midwest, they spawned an epidemic of tornadoes from Alabama to Ontario, the like of which the United States had not seen in nearly a century. At least 148 twisters touched down in twenty-four hours, killing 309 persons and injuring another 5,000. Though a tornado is likely to hit a town only once every 250 years, the day's fury was visited upon Xenia, where a huge twister roared for an agonizing 35 minutes. During each of those minutes, it wreaked $3 million worth of havoc, but Xenians counted one big blessing: the tornado devastated the schools *after* their children had been dismissed.

1978 BLIZZARD
51 dead — most severe snowstorm in Ohio history
January 26, 1978
entire state

When two low pressure systems met over southern Ohio, they precipitated a once-in-a-lifetime blizzard for the Great Lakes States. In Ohio, ten inches of new snow piled on top of the foot or so already on the ground, temperatures dropped forty degrees in a few hours, and sustained winds of fifty to seventy miles per hour whipped up white-out conditions and twenty-five foot snow drifts. Governor James Rhodes called the blast the state's worst disaster ever, and he had plenty of evidence for the claim: hundreds of thousands of people stranded without food, fuel, or electricity; the Ohio Turnpike completely shut down for the first time; the state's record-low barometric pressure (28.28 inches in Cleveland); and business, commerce, and society brought to a screeching halt. In all, the blizzard cost Ohioans some $100 million, including the National Guard's $1.19 million dollar invoice for disaster services rendered.

■ *The fifteen finest Buckeye fights, frays, and fracuses in which local belligerents, bruisers, and all manner of disputants engage in nationally noted moments of high truculence*

THE SETTLERS VS. THE TREES
After the Treaty of Greene Ville gave them the go-ahead in 1795, folks came over the mountains and down the River to make a life for themselves in Ohio. All that stood in their way was 25 million acres of trees, a forest wilderness that had already staked an ancient and natural claim to ninety-five percent of the rich land where they wanted to build homes and raise their crops and children. The settlers waged a formidable fight, virtually taking on the trees one at a time, relentlessly chopping away until they wrested a civilization out of the woods, clearing the first space for the nation's westward expansion. Remarkably, it took only a few generations for their axes to conquer the trees. But lately conservation has mimicked politics, and the old enemy is now appreciated as a valued ally — since the 1950's, Ohio forest lands have actually increased to 7.1 million acres and there are woods to be found in every county of the state.

OHIO VS. MICHIGAN
In 1835, Ohio and Michigan nearly went to war in a border dispute involving an eight-mile-wide strip of land. Both called up their militia, but President Andrew Jackson intervened and cooled the Democratic tempers of the states' governors before the conflict escalated beyond fist fights. In the end, Ohio "won" by retaining Toledo, a perfectly good terminal for a canal, the profitable prospect of which had been the real bone of contention all along. Michigan got its Upper Peninsula, and any latent hostility over the matter is now expressed on the football fields of the state universities, where the Wolverines and Buckeyes annually attempt to encroach on each others' territory.

GENERAL DENVER VS. EDWARD GILBERT
James W. Denver was raised in Clinton County, took his law degree in Cincinnati,

fought with Scott in Mexico, edited newspapers, went to California during the Gold Rush, brought law and order to the Kansas Territory as Commissioner of Indian Affairs, gave his name to the capital of Colorado, and commanded a brigade in the Civil War, all before 1866, when he opened a law office in Washington. Denver had a fine career, colorful and successful, and marred only by one incident — the death of Edward Gilbert in 1852. Gilbert, a Palo Alto newspaper editor, wrote scathing editorials about Denver's handling of supply trains during the Gold Rush. The bad blood between them escalated to a duel, and Gilbert was killed. In later years, Denver ran for Congress and the Senate, and was twice considered by the Democrats as a Presidential nominee. But the duel shadowed and thwarted his political ambitions, and Denver became, as John Gunther wrote, "an old-time governor of Kansas, whom scarcely anybody has ever heard of." Were it not for his feud with Gilbert, history might well have treated him otherwise.

THE McCOOKS VS. THE CONFEDERACY
According to one historian, the "Fighting McCooks" were the greatest family of soldiers in history, and they came to the Union in tribes headed by two brothers. The "Tribe of Dan" (Major Daniel McCook) hailed from Carrollton; The "Tribe of John" (Dr. John McCook) from Steubenville. In all, sixteen McCooks — the two brothers and their fourteen sons — went marching off to death and glory (five died, seven became generals) in the Civil War. Major Dan, who was 63 when the fighting began, perished from wounds received when the bold Confederate Morgan raided Ohio soil. Dan Jr. led the charge on Kenesaw Mountain by reciting poetry. In war, the fighting McCooks were at Vicksburg, Bull Run, Shiloh, and Sherman's March. In peace, the surviving McCooks became clergymen, Congressman, and Governor.

SHERMAN VS. THE PRESS
The newspapers said that he was crazy and incompetent, and William Tecumseh Sherman

"Cussed be Sherman, for he took Atlanta. And he marcht thro the Confedrisy, and respected not the feelins of ennybody . . . So he cavorts ez he wills, like a yearlin mule with a chestnut burr under his tale."

— Petroleum V. Nasby

In 1864, Grant and Sherman met in Cincinnati's Burnet House and hatched the plan that forever extended the limits of acceptable wartime conduct. That fall, the irascible Sherman, a pro-slaver and the Northern commander most sympathetic to the South, led sixty thousand men on a 50-60 mile wide scorched path across the Georgia countryside, stripping farms of grain and livestock, spreading dread through the population. Along the way, he became the first general to consciously demoralize a people in order to subdue its army, and the first to wreck an economy to achieve the same end. He thus became the spiritual godfather to the bomber aircraft of World War II, Hiroshima, and the search-and-destroy missions of Vietnam.

regarded reporters as perpetual flies in the Army ointment. They thought the public had a right to know; he said their stories leaked information that cost him battles and killed his men. During the Civil War, the tug-of-war between Sherman and the press resulted in the General ordering a news blackout, the first in the nation's history. At issue was the still-nagging debate over freedom of the press against the need for military secrecy. Sherman had "the dirty newspaper scribblers who have the impudence of Satan" banned from the lines and court-martialed, but he found it easier to take Atlanta than stop a war correspondent sniffing out a story. Tradition has it that Sherman refused even to shake hands with publisher Horace Greeley, but in his memoirs he conceded, "Yet so greedy are the people at large for war news, that it is doubtful whether any army commander can exclude all reporters without bringing down on himself a clamor that may imperil his own safety."

STANTON VS. PRESIDENT JOHNSON

Andrew Johnson tried to continue Lincoln's benign Reconstruction policy, but the new President was hampered by Radical Republicans who wanted to punish the defeated South. Secretary of War Edwin Stanton sympathized with the Radicals, and when Johnson fired him, the Ohio native refused to step down, locking himself in his office and claiming that under the Tenure of Office Act, only Congress could dismiss him. Stanton thus precipitated the first and only impeachment procedings against a U.S. President, giving the Radicals an excuse to oust Johnson for violating the Act. With Chief Justice Salmon Chase presiding, Johnson's 1868 trial in the Senate tested both the Act's legality and executive versus legislative powers. Johnson had everything to lose; Ohio Senator Ben Wade, as President Pro Tempore, had everything to gain. A guilty verdict would toss the White House into Wade's Radical lap. Johnson was acquitted by one vote, the federal balance of power was maintained, and Stanton, having failed to prove his point, resigned the same day.

❝ *You see, Grant stood by me when I was crazy, and I stood by him when he was drunk.* ❞

William Sherman

6 *We've got them.* **9**

Custer

VICTORIA CLAFLIN WOODHULL
VS. HENRY WARD BEECHER

She was born in Homer, Ohio, to ne'er-do-wells who sold patent medicine. But Victoria was uncommonly smart and pretty, and these assets eased the way to her becoming the first woman to run for President (against Grant in 1872), a New York stockbroker, a newspaper publisher, and an unabashed pioneer of Women's Rights and Free Love. Beecher, whose father was a pillar of Cincinnati's Calvinist community, was the most famous preacher of his day, a glib and handsome figure of liberal righteousness, who enjoyed a lucrative ministry. They clashed when Beecher's sisters — Catherine, the educator, and Harriet, the author — took umbrage with Victoria's free-thinking ways. Victoria retaliated in her newspaper in 1872, disclosing Beecher's affair with a parishioner's wife and touching off one of the nation's most notorious scandals. The aggrieved husband, who was one of Victoria's own paramours, sued Beecher for adultery. The trial was juicy, but the jury hung. Victoria escaped to England, where she lived and died in style, apparently bought off by the family of her old friend Commodore Vanderbilt. Beecher, his brilliant reputation permanently tarnished, went back to his forgiving flock. When he died in 1887, forty thousand people paid their respects, and ninety percent of them were women.

CUSTER VS. THE SIOUX

After the Army finished fighting the Rebels in the South, it took on the Indians in the West. George Armstrong Custer, who had been the boy wonder of the Civil War — the New Rumley, Ohio, native who dashed into battle with flowing hair and fancy uniforms, made general at 24, and walked away from Appomattox with the Confederate flag under his arm — got command of the U.S. Seventh Cavalry. On June 25, 1876, he led a column of some 250 men to the Little Big Horn in Montana, where they were attacked and annihilated by an estimated 4000 Sioux. Although Sitting Bull won the battle, the Sioux lost the war. Public back-

"If I were an Indian, I often think I would greatly prefer to cast my lot among those of my people who adhered to the free open plains, rather than submit to the confined limits of a reservation, there to be the recipient of the blessed benefits of civilization."

— *Custer*

lash from the massacre gave the Army a free hand to subdue the Indians, which they did within a year of Custer's infamous end, and thus his Last Stand became a permanent addition to the national mystique.

ELISHA GRAY VS. ALEXANDER GRAHAM BELL

Mr. Bell's celebrity, perhaps, obscures the fact that the *idea* for a telephone was not exclusively his. In fact, he was in the 1870's in a horse race with Belmont County native Elisha Gray to develop the apparatus, and their dash to the Patent Office ended in a photo finish, Bell arriving just hours before Gray and walking off with probably the most valuable patent ever granted. But Gray, the brilliant co-founder of Western Electric, did not trot benignly off to inventors' pasture. He charged Bell and the patent examiner with collusion, and the case went to the Supreme Court, where it was dismissed. For the rest of his days, Gray felt cheated by the hands of the clock, writing bitterly, "The history of the phone will never be fully written. It is partly hidden away in twenty or thirty thousand pages of testimony and partly lying in the hearts and consciences of a few whose lips are sealed . . ."

RUTHERFORD B. HAYES VS. SAMUEL TILDEN

The election of 1876 was the most controversial Presidential contest in the nation's history. Democrat Tilden of New York defeated Republican Hayes of Ohio by a healthy margin in the popular vote and led in the electoral college vote. But the votes of several states were disputed, putting the electoral count in question until January, when Congress appointed a bipartisan commission to settle the deadlock. In what has become known as the Compromise of 1877, the Democrats agreed to award Hayes the Presidency, if the Republicans would promise to remove federal troops from the South. Hayes thus "stole" the election from Tilden, whose outraged supporters threatened to get him the White House by force. Hayes, who was stuck with the sobriquet "His Fraudulency," kept his part of the bargain in the Great

"Fighting battles is like courting girls: those who make the most pretensions and are the boldest usually win."
— *Hayes*

Swap. As President, he withdrew the troops, effectively ending Reconstruction and the federal effort to force black civil rights in the South.

WILLIAM McKINLEY VS. SPAIN

When McKinley became President, the United States was the fiesty, confident new kid in the neighborhood of nations. Spain, on the other hand, was a dowager Empress, an aging, ailing matriarch still working to support her farflung colonial children. Many Americans sympathized with the Cubans who were fighting to free themselves from Spain's long apron strings. When the U.S. battleship *Maine* suspiciously blew up in Havana harbor in 1898, McKinley, egged on by the yellow press, sent Teddy Roosevelt and Commodore Dewey to give the feeble old girl a kick that knocked her off her empire. The Spanish-American conflict was exactly as John Hay described it — a "splendid little war" that in only four months and with few battlefield casualties thrust Cuba, Guam, Puerto Rico, and the Philippines into the open arms of the United States. McKinley's donnybrook with Spain made the U.S. a world power, and an imperialistic one at that, which also quickly acquired Hawaii and Wake Island, and after the diplomatic Mr. Hay opened the door, sent troops to China during the Boxer Rebellion.

ORVILLE WRIGHT VS. THE SMITHSONIAN

Early in the century, the Smithsonian sponsored Samuel Langley's experimental, and expensive, flights in the *Aerodrome,* an unsatisfactory craft that dunked him in the Potomac. A few years later, Smithsonian Secretary Charles Walcott maintained that the *Aerodrome* rather than the 1903 Wright *Flyer* gave the world powered flight. Orville Wright hotly protested, but Walcott would not budge, whereupon the surviving Brother shipped his *Flyer* off to the London Science Museum. There *The Flyer* stayed for twenty years, until Walcott's successor acknowledged Dayton's Wright Brothers as the true inventors of the airplane. In 1948, the Wright estate sold the

"The truth is I didn't want the Philippines, and when they came to us as a gift from the gods, I did not know what to do with them . . . and one night late it came to me . . . that there was nothing left for us to do but to take them all and to educate the Filipinos and uplift and civilize and Christianize them, and by God's grace do the very best we could by them . . ."
— *McKinley*

Flyer to the Smithsonian for one dollar, with the proviso that the airplane always be prominently displayed and credited with being the world's first successful airplane.

CLARENCE DARROW VS. WILLIAM JENNINGS BRYAN

When John Scopes answered the call of the ACLU to teach evolution in violation of Tennessee law, he set in motion one of this century's most famous arguments, the great debate between Darrow and Bryan in the 1925 "monkey trial." Darrow, who was born in Kinsman and had practiced corporate law in Youngstown, was the most famous criminal lawyer in America. He had defended Eugene Debs and Leopold and Loeb, and now he championed Scope's right to present a biological theory in the public schools. When Tennessee hired silver-tongued William Jennings Bryan as a prosecutor, the trial quickly became a contest between science and religion, the acerbic agnostic Darrow matching wits with the verbose fundamentalist Bryan. Their debate climaxed when Bryan took the witness stand and Darrow quizzed him on his literal interpretation of the Bible. Technically, Darrow lost. Scopes was found guilty, although he got off with a slap-on-the wrist fine. But the strain of the trial killed Bryan, and Darrow, with his uncanny ability to focus public attention on a national social issue, had triumphed once again.

HARRY TRUMAN VS. YOUNGSTOWN SHEET AND TUBE

In 1952, the Steelworkers of America threatened to strike for higher wages, and President Truman, fearing a walkout during the Korean War, declared a national emergency and seized the steel mills in his capacity as Commander-in-Chief. Charles Sawyer, the Cincinnati attorney who was Truman's Secretary of Commerce, suddenly found himself in charge of sixty-eight steel mills and their 600,000 workers. The mill owners, of course, cried foul, and selected a steel company in Youngstown to lead the legal fight against Truman. The case went to the Supreme Court as Youngstown Sheet & Tube Company vs. Sawyer, and the Justices with truly deliberate speed ruled that Truman's takeover was unconstitutional, a landmark decision that placed the strongest ties on the hands of a President until the Watergate era.

GOODYEAR VS. GOLDSMITH

In 1986, the very existence of Akron's Goodyear Tire and Rubber Company was threatened by international financier Sir James Goldsmith, one of the "corporate raiders" who make their profits on paper instead of production. Sir James and Goodyear CEO Robert Mercer went eyeball to eyeball, and the Brit blinked. With the city cheering on, Goodyear "sent the limey bastard home" all right, but it was a costly victory. In order to save the corporate body, the company had to sacrifice a limb, and Goodyear Aerospace — the nation's time-honored blimp builder and a major employer in Akron — was sold to raise the cash to buy him off. In appreciation for Akron's steadfast support, Mercer broke tradition and named the company's latest, and possibly last, blimp *The Spirit of Akron.*

"I've got my bundle."
— *Sir James Goldsmith*

Rubber hose — in Akron in the 1870's, B.F. Goodrich made the elastic, durable hoses that radically improved firefighting and were eventually adapted into all manner of places, from gardens to operating rooms.

Incandescent lightbulb — Milan's Thomas Edison ushered in the Age of Electricity by patenting a practical lightbulb in 1879, then developed a central system to power it, revolutionizing life and work in America.

Phonograph — Edison invented a device for recording dictation in the 1870's, never anticipating that it would put music from Bach to rock in living rooms and launch the home entertainment industry.

Grocery bag — thanks to supermarkets, Americans annually use billions of the freestanding, flat-bottomed brown paper bags that Fremont native Charles Stilwell designed and manufactured in 1883.

Ore unloader — Conneaut's George Hulett mechanized the laborious transfer of iron ore from ships to freight cars in 1898, a transportation boon that expedited the growth of America's steel industry.

Airplane — Dayton's Orville and Wilbur Wright unlocked the secret of powered flight by controlling yaw, pitch, and roll, a 1903 achievement that forever shrank time and distance.

Book matches — Ohio Columbus Barber's Diamond Match Company in Barberton put fire conveniently in people's pockets, designing the modern matchbook and making match tips safe by introducing nonpoisonous sesquisulfide in 1911.

Automobile self-starter — Daytonian Charles Kettering started a car with an electric motor in 1911, rendering the cumbersome hand crank obsolete and allowing women to get comfortably, and permanently, behind the wheel.

Continuous rolled steel — in Middletown during World War I, John Tytus made strips of sheet steel, a discovery that raised the standard of living by lowering prices on consumer goods from bicycles to Buicks.

Formica — in 1913, Cincinnati's Herbert Faber and Daniel O'Connor developed an electrical insulation substitute for mica; today, the practical plastic laminate adorns virtually every kitchen and bathroom in America.

Traffic light — in 1923, Clevelander Garrett Morgan enhanced America's love affair with the automobile, giving intersections the ubiquitous additions of (1) automatic "stop" and "go" lights, and (2) the yellow "caution" signal.

Refrigerated box car — Cincinnati-born electrician Frederick McKinley Jones revolutionized food transportation and the American diet in 1940, when he found a practical way to keep railroad cars and trucks cold.

Microencapsulation — in 1953, Barrett Green developed in Dayton a process that controlled chemical release, ultimately giving the world such amenities as time-released medication and carbonless copy paper.

Disposable diapers — this 1962 invention from Cincinnati's Procter & Gamble alleviated parenthood's nastiest chore, made families more mobile, and while a mixed environmental blessing, still gives a fresh start to an estimated three-fourths of the nation's babies.

Liquid crystal display — in 1971, Daytonian John Janning solved the elusive problem of permanently aligning liquid crystal molecules; his process made possible those small wonders of the world, digital watches and pocket calculators.

■ *Several of Ohio's very best four-legged and fine-feathered friends, who have run, romped, trotted, kicked, swung, swum, grunted, and jabbered their way into our hearts, minds, and history*

THE CONWAY MASTODON

When the glaciers retreated ten thousand years ago, hairy elephant-like animals called mastodons walked the frozen land we know now as Ohio. Victims of both prehistoric hunters and changes in climate and vegetation, the mastodons died off and left their huge skeletons. In 1894, one of the most complete and largest male mastodon skeletons ever found was unearthed on the farm of N.S. Conway in Clark County, a prodigious specimen now displayed at the Ohio Historical Center, Columbus.

THE CINCINNATI PIGS

Between 1818 and 1851, Ohioans perfected the art and science of letting their corn walk to market, the walking being done by pigs and the market being Cincinnati. Slaughterhouses in America's *first* hog butcher to the world annually produced enough pork to circle the world in sausage, twice.

GARLICK'S TROUT

Theodatus Garlick, the multi-talented surgeon, scientist, artist, and innovator who was the Benjamin Franklin of nineteenth century Cleveland, was also an enthusiastic angler who became the first person in the United States to artificially breed fish. In 1853, he fertilized trout eggs in vitro, the culmination of experiments that had also resulted in his building the nation's first fish hatchery. In 1857, Garlick published his findings in the *Ohio Farmer,* a treatise which laid the foundation for U.S. fish farming.

CRUISER

The "most vicious stallion in England" cemented the international reputation of John Solomon Rarey, the Ohioan who was one of the finest horse trainers that the world has ever known. Cruiser was such a living fury that the lord who owned him put up a hundred pounds against the horse being tamed in three months, but Rarey accomplished the feat in a day. He became the toast of Europe's horse-loving aristocracy and in 1860 returned to Groveport a rich man, accompanied by the now-famous Cruiser, and immortalized in newly coined word, rareyfy, meaning "to tame a horse by kindness."

PRIVATE TRUST
A mongrel of vaguely spaniel parentage, he was the first dog mustered in and out of the U.S. Army, being in 1862 in the possession of Private Samuel Shannon, who enlisted himself and his canine in the Union cause, whence both served under Grant in the Wilderness campaign, the man in artillery and the beast as Watch Dog. After the war, Shannon became a nurseryman in Troy, where Trust retired from active duty, his discharge papers having been duly recorded in the Miami County courthouse.

JACK
When coal baron Jacob Heatherington built his mansion in Bellaire in 1870, he declared it the "House that Jack Built," Jack being the mule who unfailingly toiled beside him as he rose from rags to riches in the Belmont County coal banks. Old Jake said he couldn't have done it without Jack, and the first guest in the house was the approving mule, whose image was carved in relief over the doorway.

CRESCEUS
Since Ohio is the nation's harness racing center, the standardbred reigns supreme, a venerable dynasty distinguished at the turn of the century by the world-famous trotter from Toledo. Cresceus held seventeen world records simultaneously, including the one that he set in Columbus when he did a mile in 2.04 seconds in 1900.

MARTHA
The last remaining member of the species *Ectopistes migratorius*, the passenger pigeon, she

died September 1, 1914, at the Cincinnati Zoo. Once one of the earth's most populous species, the passenger pigeons were mercilessly hunted into extinction in only a hundred years, and Martha's death was a cruel landmark, the first time mankind could document the passing of a species.

RALPH

When he was born in Cincinnati in 1987, Ralph was called a "scientific milestone," the first non-native species born of a domestic animal. Though Ralph is an Indian gaur, the "mother" who received him as a transplanted embryo was a Holstein. His extraordinary birth resulted from the pioneering work of the Cincinnati Wildlife Research Federation, which seeks to save endangered species through its "frozen zoo" of embryos and semen.

BALTO

Balto, a Siberian malamute sled dog, became the hero of Alaska in the hard winter of 1925, when the city of Nome was seized by a diphtheria epidemic and serum had to be transported by dog sled. Balto led his team through blizzard conditions in a 150 mile race with death that the dogs won with their eyes frozen shut. Afterwards, the team became imperiled, probably destined for the carnival circuit until Clevelanders came to the rescue and raised money for the dogs' peaceable future at Brookside Zoo. Balto, who died there in 1933, is now mounted at Cleveland's Museum of Natural History.

SUSIE

She was the world's first trained gorilla, and she came via a first class ticket on the *Graf Zeppelin* to Cincinnati, where from 1931 to her death in 1947, she resided in a four-room apartment in the zoo, fitting accommodations since the civilized Susie knew how to properly use a knife and fork and unfailingly shared her food with her trainer. Susie's birthday always occasioned greetings and presents from around the nation, and the celebration in 1936 set a zoo attendance record.

FELIX CATUS

He lived in perhaps the only cat house ever designed by Frank Lloyd Wright. In the 1950's, the eminent architect designed a house for a Cincinnati couple, whose little girl also wanted him to build one for her pet cat. He obliged, and three decades later, Felix's angular house had enough Wright stuff to sell for $10,000.

COLO

She was the first gorilla born in captivity, a three-pound, five-ounce landmark for the Columbus Zoo in 1956. There, Colo also became the matriarch of the nation's first four-generation gorilla family, when her great-granddaughter Cora was born in 1979.

RAMBLING WILLIE

His harness race showings were so poor that Willie might have ended up in the glue factory had his owner not pledged to tithe the standardbred's future winnings to her church in West Mansfield in 1973. From then on, Willie was a winner. In 1983, in fact, he was the winningest standardbred horse of all time — earning more than $2 million dollars, ten percent of which faithfully went to the church's collection plate.

SCHOTTZIE

Ohio's most famous St. Bernard belongs to Cincinnati Reds owner Marge Schott, who has made her beloved pet the team's unofficial, and omnipresent, mascot. Schottzie, a singularly personable pup whose name puns the German word for sweetheart, has made myriad personal appearances for the Reds, including network TV with David Letterman.

CHIEF

Another veteran of the Letterman show, Chief grew, literally, into the national spotlight in 1987, when he won for the second year in a row the Ohio State Fair's Buckeye Big Boar Contest by weighing in at 1205 pounds. Twice as big as the average breeding hog, Chief got used to throwing his weight around in his hometown of North Lewisburg.

SCIPIO

Orville Wright's beloved St. Bernard kept the Grand Old Man of Aviation company in his Dayton mansion after Brother Wilbur died. Since Sister Katharine was a Latin teacher, Scipio probably got his name from the old Roman who conquered Hannibal. In any event, this Scipio conquered Orville, who took more photographs of the dog than his aviation trophies and carried the canine's likeness in his wallet to his dying day.

Scipio

"A few weeks before his father died, Orville brought home a St. Bernard puppy. He named it Scipio. Over the months and years, Scipio's weight increased from sixteen pounds to one hundred sixty, but like many large dogs, he suffered from rheumatism and his life was a short one as dogs' lives go. Orville did not take many photographs in his later years, but in the collection of photos made from the Wright Brothers' glass-plate negatives in the Library of Congress there are no fewer than ten pictures of Scipio, one of which Orville carried in his wallet until the day he died. He had a soft heart for the big, rheumatic dog, having suffered from sciatic pains himself ever since his accident at Fort Myer in 1908 . . ."
— *Wilbur and Orville,*
Fred Howard

■ *Step right up for a sampling of commercial statesmen, the boosters, pitchmen, con men, and promoters, who with some luck and great pluck hawked their wares and wherewithal across Ohio and the nation*

WILLIAM DUER, JOEL BARLOW, AND WILLIAM PLAYFAIR

In Paris, they promised a land of milk and honey along the Ohio — eighty pound catfish, grapes so great that streams ran red with wine, and the certain prospect that "Gallipolis" would be the future capital of the United States. Five hundred Frenchmen snapped up deeds in 1790, but instead of a paradise in the wilderness, they found a wilderness in the wilderness. Alas, Mr. Playfair had not lived up to his name, for the Scioto Company land swindle ranks with paying the Indians glass beads for Manhattan.

CASSIE CHADWICK

Her 1905 trial attracted international attention, for the star witness against her was none other than Andrew Carnegie. On the bold, but thin claim of being the famous industrialist's illegitimate daughter, "the greatest adventuress in the world" had bilked Cleveland's foremost financiers out of an estimated $20 million. Mrs. Chadwick was convicted and died in the Ohio State Penitentiary, but her con had been fun while it lasted: she bought diamonds by the muff full and her Euclid Avenue manse was a monument to conspicuous consumption.

THE IMMORTAL J.N. FREE

His surname was his excuse, for in the late 1800's, Ohio's most notorious freeloader rode the rails gratis from town to town on sheer nerve and a gift for gab. In top hat and tails, the self-styled "Demostenes of America" considered his flowery orations fair exchange for room and board. When a frustrated hotelier offered to forget half his bill in exchange for immediate payment, the Immortal J.N. waved his cane and announced that he would be equally generous and forget the other half.

THE GARVER BROTHERS

Dad told them "to go to the limit to please the customer," and Rudy and Albert took his advice so well that in the middle of the Depression their Strasburg country store grossed half a million dollars a year. They sent employees to plow for sick farmers, carried so many suits of clothing that customers had to climb ladders to see them all, sponsored spelling bees and baking contests, had a man walking day and night on a mattress in their front window, and hired a Santa Claus who could juggle *and* walk a tightrope. After Albert compiled one of the nation's first direct mail lists, he laid claim to 12,000 regular customers — 7,000 of whom he knew by name.

MARK HANNA

He is credited with selling William McKinley to the nation. A Cleveland industrialist turned kingmaker, Hanna believed that what was good for business was good for America and determined to advance that theory by putting "his boy" in the White House. McKinley, with his "statesman's face," provided the perfect vehicle, and Hanna provided the rest: a multimillion-dollar war chest, a horde of speechwriters and campaigners, and 300 tons of McKinley political propaganda.

SAMUEL BRUBAKER HARTMAN

Dr. Hartman was an itinerant "advertising physician," a euphemism for patent medicine man. He invented an elixir called Peruna, and by 1906, his Columbus factory was bottling the best-selling medication in the nation. Peruna's popularity, no doubt, started with its being thirty percent alcohol. The good Doctor poured his profits into a "farm" just south of the city: a 5000 acre extravaganza with 700 employees, a private railroad, a hotel, "every branch of agriculture and stock raising," and forty miles of fences to contain it all. "It was," said one observer, "like the State Fair every day."

JIM TARBELL

The baroque Mr. Tarbell holds forth in Arnold's, Cincinnati's oldest saloon and unoffi-

"Mark Hanna was the personification of our commercial age — the age of building, planting, reaping; of ships on ocean, and on land, steel highways and the rolling wheels of trade . . ."
— Indiana Senator A.J. Beveridge, 1904

cial town hall. In earlier days, he played reveille on his trombone out front, answered by a bugle-blowing art dealer from across the street. As one of the nation's great saloon keepers, Tarbell has graduated to various causes near to his downtown heart, namely the poor but beautiful Over-the-Rhine neighborhood. Originally a rock concert promoter, he now stages events, benefits, and curiosities, all of them promoting, finally, Cincinnati.

BARNEY KROGER

Advertise, advertise, advertise. When Barney Kroger went into the grocery business in Cincinnati in the 1880's, he was one of the first to bombard the public with print advertising. His low prices brought in customers in droves, and their sheer volume caused a chain reaction: a string of stores that not only made him one of the nation's foremost grocers but also still survives him by half a century.

THE LAZARUS FAMILY

With lively marketing techniques that are now standard department store procedures, four generations of this family of Columbus and Cincinnati retailers built local emporiums into a national merchandising *tour de force,* Federated Department Stores. From drawing a crowd with alligators and free lemonade to innovations such as the bargain basement, no-down-payment credit, and grouping racks of clothing by size instead of price, they were masters at drumming up business and the truest of merchant princes.

PROCTER & GAMBLE

Since candlemaker William Procter and soapmaker James Gamble teamed up in 1837, they have been guests in virtually every American home, thanks to the merchandising magic worked by the Cincinnati company they founded. Procter & Gamble products are not just household names; to a large extent, they *define* the American household of the late twentieth century. In kitchen, bath, and laundry, Procter & Gamble brands — from Duncan Hines to Charmin to Tide — dominate.

> *Costs are up, spirits are down. We must regenerate our dancing feet and our sense of humor.*

Jim Tarbell
and Whistles

Ivory soap, one of the company's most venerable products, was named from a passage in the Forty-fifth Psalm, but divine intervention does not explain Procter & Gamble's long and spectacular track record. It stays one step ahead of competitors with a time-honored tactic, the consumer advertising blitz. If the nation's door is always open to Procter & Gamble products, it is probably because the company is always knocking: since 1963, Procter & Gamble has spent more on advertising than any other company in the nation.

JOHN D. ROCKEFELLER

He systematically monopolized the nation's oil industry by process of elimination — any and all competition, that is. Although the billionaire thought God gave him his money, most folks opined that it came from his infamous Standard Oil trust. When Rockefeller started handing out dimes to Cleveland street urchins, his image improved considerably. By the time he died in 1937, his philanthropy had escalated to funding universities and foundations to the tune of some 600 million ballyhooed dollars, which forever fixed his name — in both the cement and subconscious of the nation — as a synonym for fabulous wealth.

JACOB SAPIRSTEIN

In 1906, he humbly penned his own job description and put it on the wagon that served as his horse-drawn storefront: "Jacob Sapirstein, Jobber of Postcards, Leaflets and Folders." Sapirstein lived a Horatio Alger story Cleveland-style, building a one-man operation into the giant American Greetings Corporation by latching on to new product ideas (greeting cards) and licensed characters (Holly Hobbie, Strawberry Shortcake). When he died in 1987, it took 23,000 employees around the world to carry on his entrepreneurial legacy.

"PEANUT JIM" SHELTON

He was one of the most colorful sideshows in all of baseball. Shelton always wore a top hat to Cincinnati Reds games, and in that outrageous but unforgettable garb, he hawked his

"Instead of spending money on amusements, my employees will be given an opportunity to add to their savings."
— *John D. Rockefeller on why he made folks labor on Labor Day*

"John D. Rockefeller is mad about money, though sane in everything else."
— *Mark Hanna*

way from the obscurity of a peanut pushcart to the immortality of having a stadium walk named in his honor. Always the salesman, Shelton once foiled a mugger by selling the rogue some peanuts, and after 1979, when he lost his legs at age 90, the indefatigable Shelton took to vending from his wheelchair.

"I'm sure I would have liked Cincinnati much better had the people not dealt largely in hogs . . ."
— *Frances Trollope, 1830's*

FRANCES TROLLOPE
In the 1820's, this down-on-her-luck English-woman hatched a plan: she was going to expose Cincinnati to the finer things and, in return, the raw boom town was going to make her rich. When her fancy emporium flopped, she carved out a lucrative career of Cincinnati-bashing, resourcefully turning her diary into *The Domestic Manners of the Americans*, a phenomenally successful book whose clever, candid sketches of the first ugly Americans are still widely quoted.

WILLIAM NEEDHAM WHITELEY
He invented a mechanical reaper and held 100 other patents; his enterprise made him the "Reaper King" and Springfield "The Champion City," and in the 1880's, his forty-four acre factory was second in size only to the Krupp arms company in Germany. But before he could sell his reaper to the world, Whiteley had to sell it to Springfield, which required his full powers of persuasion. He unhitched a team of horses and by himself pulled the reaper across a field — running.

LA CHOY
As the nation's leading producers of Chinese food, La Choy has pulled off an incredible merchandising coup: convincing America that egg rolls emanate from the fields surrounding Archbold, Ohio.

■ *Ten grand plans gone awry, good intentions that Ohioans sent up on the rocket of hope and glory, but which sank like a stone into the obscurity of false starts and lost causes*

THE LAKE ERIE-OHIO RIVER CANAL

A hundred and fifty years after canals went out of fashion, this one survives in the realm of possibility, a vast territory where dreams and ambition feed on a steady diet of tantalizing precepts, all of which begin with would, could, should, and the ever-popular if. *If,* for example, says one canal booster, the project had been built twenty years ago, the steel industry would still be alive and well in Cleveland and Youngstown. But alas, the canal does not exist, though many plans for it do. Every generation or so since George Washington first proposed it, the idea of the canal has risen phoenix-like from the ashes of hard times. One of the latest yea-sayers is a Congressman from Youngstown. He wants to dig a 100-to-120 mile canal from near Cleveland to East Liverpool on the Ohio River, but the $5 billion-plus price tag continues to daunt modern true believers.

THE CONVICTION OF EUGENE DEBS

The foundations of the mighty bulwark that is the First Amendment crumbled a bit in a Cleveland courtroom in 1918, when the Espionage Act was very loosely invoked to silence Eugene Debs, an impassioned labor organizer and Socialism's most eloquent and visible spokesman. He was arrested after making an anti-war, pro-social justice speech in Canton, and the government's case hinged largely on his statement of philosophy: "The master class has always declared the war, the subject class has always fought it." The jury found him guilty of trying to incite disloyalty, obstructing recruitment into the armed forces, and encouraging resistance to the U.S. government. He was sentenced to a decade behind bars, and the following year, the Supreme Court upheld his conviction. But Debs, an indefatigable Presidential candidate, ran again on the 1920 Socialist ticket as Convict #2273, coming in a distant third behind two Ohioans, Republican Warren G.

"I have no country to fight for; my country is the earth, and I am a citizen of the world."
— *Debs*

Harding and Democrat James M. Cox. Ultimately, however, the Cleveland trial proved a failure, for the Bill of Rights triumphed after all. In 1921, President Harding surprised the nation by bowing to the principle of Free Speech and pardoning Debs, ordering him sent home in time to spend Christmas with his family.

THE LAKE ERIE CONSPIRACY
During the Civil War, thousands of Southern officers were imprisoned on Lake Erie's Johnson's Island, and in 1864, Confederate agents devised a grand plan to free them. Charles H. Cole and John Yeats Beall were to hijack the *U.S.S. Michigan* and use the gunboat's weapons to blast away at the island while the prisoners escaped. The plot fell to pieces when the conspirators bungled their rendezvous on Lake Erie. Beall, who with the help of mercenary Bennet Burley had commandered the Detroit-to-Sandusky steamer *Philo Parsons,* found the vessel so short of fuelwood that he had to turn back, while Cole managed to get himself arrested aboard the *Michigan.* Though Cole was eventually freed, Beall was hanged. As for Burley, he cooled his heels in jail while lawyers debated whether charging him with war crimes would constitute formal U.S. recognition of the Confederacy. Finally, Burley was tried in Port Clinton for robbing *Philo Parsons* passengers. But before the jury reached a verdict, Burley broke out of jail by climbing down an apple tree. He left a farewell note on top of a Bible for the overly trusting local sheriff: "Sunday — I have gone out for a walk — perhaps I will return shortly." Burley never did return. He went to England, where he turned from fighting wars to reporting them and made a name for himself as a foreign correspondent for the *London Daily Telegraph.*

ARTHUR ST. CLAIR
It is said that President Washington was having dinner when he received word that General St. Clair had just suffered the worst defeat ever meted out by the Indians to a white army. Washington controlled his anger until his

guests departed, then launched into a tirade against his old Revolutionary War crony. He had specifically warned St. Clair about the wily skill of the wilderness Indians, yet the gouty general still bumbled into an ambush by thinking he was in Indiana when he actually was a good sixty miles away near present-day Fort Recovery. St. Clair lost 630 soldiers to Blue Jacket and Little Turtle that November, 1791, and the costliness of his error was compounded by three more years of frontier bloodshed until Mad Anthony Wayne finally subdued the Indians. In truth, the aristocratic, ailing St. Clair was ill-suited to lead his ragtag army of poorly-paid, poorly-equipped men into battle. A congressional investigation later exonerated him for the defeat, but that battle ("the most shocking that has happened in America since its first Discovery") was the turning point of his fortunes, financial and political. Though St. Clair had nobly mortgaged his own property to help finance the American Revolution, he stubbornly clung to his elitist Federalist beliefs during his fourteen years as Governor of the Northwest Territory. Meanwhile, the pioneer population increasingly favored the "liberal" Democratic Republicans who wanted rule by the common man. In 1802, the crusty Governor foolishly made a vitriolic speech against President Jefferson, who had no choice but to fire him on the eve of the Ohio statehood that St. Clair had long opposed. He then retired to life as an innkeeper in Pennsylvania, where he died impoverished in 1818.

THE HOLLOW EARTH THEORY

In 1818, John Cleves Symmes, who had distinguished himself in the War of 1812, announced "To all the World" that the earth was hollow. He theorized that the center of the earth was composed of concentric spheres that could be reached through vast openings at each pole. Symmes stated that the earth's interior was a "warm and rich land, stocked with thrifty vegetables and animals, if not men . . ." Pledging his life to his theory and succored by a report certifying his sanity, Symmes sought backers for an expedition to sail over the polar lip and into the bowels of the earth where he would meet with mankind's subterranean cousins. His followers planned to call the inner Earth "Symmzonia," but they were repeatedly disappointed when Congress rejected Symmes's appeals for money. He died in 1829, but his theory lingered for nearly another hundred years until debunked by the first flights over the poles. Symmes is buried in Hamilton, where a hollow sphere marks his grave.

THE CROSLEY

When the Crosley flopped, it broke Powel Crosley Jr.'s heart. The automobile was his first business failure, and Crosley, a Cincinnati inventor who had parlayed his affinity for gadgets into a major industry, was quite accustomed to success. In the Twenties, his company not only was the world's largest manufacturer of radios, but also introduced a slew of popular "no frills" appliances, including the Shelvador, the first refrigerator with shelves on the door. Along the way, he started radio station WLW in Cincinnati. With 500,000 watts, the grossly overpowered station could be heard from the Arctic Circle to the Gulf of Mexico and was picked up on bed springs at places in between. Crosley also bought the Cincinnati Reds, the vehicle wherein he brought night baseball to the major leagues in 1935. Four years later, he debuted his ill-fated auto at the New York World's Fair. In keeping with his basic, easy-on-the-pocketbook product line, the snub-nosed Crosley came in only three colors. But at $325, the Crosley was the cheapest car on the market, and Depression-minded consumers were quite happy to put up with hand-operated windshield wipers to get fifty miles to the gallon. But after World War II, America's automotive tastes shifted toward the long and luxurious, and the no-nonsense Crosley became an idea whose time had passed, twenty years before it might have arrived with Arab oil embargos. Consumers turned a deaf ear to Mr. Crosley's exhortation, "Why take a battleship to cross the Hudson?" and he manufactured his last car in 1952.

"In one of the greatest Cincinnati sports 'sells,' silver-tongued Larry MacPhail talked industrial pioneer Crosley into buying the nearly bankrupt Reds franchise. Crosley, a Cincinnati loyalist, never regretted it, although it was reported that more than one of his wives did. His was a long, benevolent reign that kept the team at home even, it was said, in the face of a $7 million offer from New York."

— The Cincinnati Game

YOUNG TOM EDISON'S EXPERIMENTS
At the tenderest of ages, the boy who would one day give the world the gift of light on demand, was already experimenting, often to the consternation of folks in his native Milan. At the age of six, Edison set fire to his father's barn "to see what would happen." He soon found out. The fire got out of hand and turned the barn to ashes, whereupon young Edison learned that the price of a failed experiment was a public whipping. Another time, he tried to make one of his chums lighter than air. Edison assured the lad that if he downed a mixture of water and a bicarbonate laxative, the resulting gas bubbles would float him to the ceiling. But instead of going up, the poor boy was soon down with a severe stomachache.

THE ROSE MARY STRETCH
In 1943, Rose Mary Woods left the small town of Sebring to seek her fortune in the big city of Washington, D.C. There she found a rising star, Richard Nixon. Woods signed on as his personal secretary and remained with Nixon while he advanced from Congress to the White House. Even during the Watergate scandal her admirable loyalty never wavered. She took responsibility for gaps in Nixon's tape recorded telephone conversations by claiming that she accidentally made the erasures. According to Miss Woods, her "terrible mistake" occurred when she pressed her foot down on the advance pedal for some six minutes while simultaneously pushing the record button and reaching to answer the telephone. This remarkable physical feat was later discounted when electronics experts testified that blanks in the tape resulted from several separate erasures.

THE OHIO-INDIANA BORDER
A provision of the Northwest Ordinance of 1787 was that the Northwest Territory's first principal meridian was to run due north from the point where the Miami River meets the Ohio. The meridian marking the Ohio-Indiana border was supposed to be established by astronomical observations based on the North Star, but Congress became impatient to sell

the land about the same time that the surveyors got tired of dodging mosquitos and hostile Indians. Expediency triumphed over accuracy, and unreliable compass measurements were used. As a result, Ohio lost about one hundred square miles of land to its neighbor on the west, and the Ohio-Indiana border is the only principal meridian in the nation that is crooked.

THE BLENNERHASSETTS

Harman and Margaret Blennerhassett were Irish aristocrats, and they were also uncle and niece. The stigma of their union drove them from their native land to America, where they found another emerald isle located in the Ohio River near Marietta. There in 1800, they built a grand estate and lived, appropriately, like lords in one of the largest homes in America, a seven thousand square foot Palladian mansion complemented by formal gardens and maintained by a retinue of servants. And then in 1805, the great scoundrel of American politics, Aaron Burr, who only the year before had killed his old rival Alexander Hamilton in a duel, involved the Blennerhassetts in a disastrous scheme. He convinced the couple to help finance his plan to seize a chunk of the Louisiana Purchase for his own private empire, promising to reward them with lucrative and powerful positions in his new nation. When President Jefferson got wind of the plot, Burr and Blennerhassett were arrested for treason. Though a sensational trial acquitted both men, the Blennerhassetts' foolish trust in Burr had ruined them. Their fortune was lost, their mansion was sacked, and their disgrace was irreparable. For the rest of their lives, they drifted from place to place, vainly trying to reestablish themselves. Ironically, they both died, broke and broken, on islands — Harman on Guernsey in 1831, and Margaret on Manhattan eleven years later.

"Margaret Blennerhassett became popular right away — at least among the men. The saying in the neighborhood was that the young men would work for a full day but just take a half-day's wages for the privilege of looking at Mrs. Blennerhassett . . ."
    — Ray Swick, historian

■ *The twelve most redoubtable Ohio perform-*
ers, Buckeye understudies who soon graduated
to the nation's larger stages and, from sawdust
to Shakespeare, became America's players

THEDA BARA

She was the original vamp, and her seductive roles in silent films created enough of a sensation to make the word a mainstay of the American vernacular, and William Fox into a motion picture mogul. Between 1916 and 1921, Bara made forty films. In contrast to the sunny, innocent heroines of the day, Fox typecast her as a dark and sultry female vampire who preyed on men . . . and *enjoyed* it. Her suggestive performances in *A Fool There Was*, *Cleopatra*, and *Vampire*, were roundly denounced by clergymen and housewives, but audiences loved the sexual fantasy. Of course, such an alluring actress demanded an exotic personal life, and the Fox Company announced that she was descended from a Middle East potentate and that her name meant "Arab death." In truth, the seductress some critics called the first publicity-made movie star was Theodosia Goodman, a nice Jewish girl from Cincinnati, a tailor's daughter who once recited "Sheridan's Ride" in amateur shows. By 1930, the vamp heyday was over, and when Bara found herself being cast in caricatures of her screen self, she retired and remained a silent legend until her death in Los Angeles in 1955.

CLYDE BEATTY

Lions and tigers are the oil and water of animal acts. They simply do not mix. But in 1926, Clyde Beatty took an unprecedented risk, bottling the natural animosity of forty lions and tigers in the same cage at the same time. His feat has yet to be surpassed, even though at the time, Beatty was probably the youngest wild animal tamer in the nation. He was born in 1903 in Bainbridge, where he saw his first circus at age seven, promptly became smitten enough to stage his own "wild animal show" with guinea pigs and a raccoon, and when he was a teenager, predictably ran away from home to join the nearest mud show. His early

"Kiss me, my fool."
— Theda Bara sub-
title, A Fool
There Was, *1916*

on-the-job training was with bears, and when a bruin attacked him, Beatty punched him in the snout, sending the bear into a backward somersault. No one then realized that a bear could do *that*, and thus Beatty accidentally invented the trick that is now a circus standard. He preferred wild cats to those born in captivity. He considered them livelier, smarter, and naive about humans, so Beatty could show them who was boss right from the start. Establishing dominance was the key to his work, and during his forty years in the ring, he became the foremost practitioner of the *en ferocite* act, a very American style that featured "fighting" cats in contrast to Europe's tableaux, or still, performances. Beatty was a first class showman, and his theatrics — the Great White Hunter costume, whip and chair, and popping pistol — added a whole new dimension to circus entertainment.

WILLIAM BOYD

He was the King of the Horse Operas, and his unlikely crown was a ten gallon hat. Yet the man who played Hopalong Cassidy with enormous success in the western serials had humble origins in Hendrysburg, Ohio, where he was born a laborer's son in 1895. His good looks made him a matinee idol in silent pictures, but both his fame and his fortune were sinking fast when he took the part of Hopalong in a B-movie in 1935. The Hopalong Cassidy movies were based on a rough-and-tough pulp character created by Clarence Mulford. But Boyd insisted on changing Hopalong for the movies, transforming a cuss into a prince in boots who always triumphed over evil. Hopalong's trademark might have been his black costume, but his soul was lily white. He never drank, smoked, swore, rolled dice, or kissed a girl. Well, he did give one lady a peck, but that was only on the forehead. And only because she was dying. In fact, Hopalong was such a noble fellow that the serials originated the much-copied "trio western," which used three heroes instead of one — Boyd was the Good Guy, a younger actor for the love interest, and an eccentric sidekick for comic relief. The concept

"I believe my voice irritates lions and tigers, so I whistle instead. I'm the world's only whistling tiger trainer."
— *Clyde Beatty*

worked so well that by 1950, Boyd was on the cover of *Time*. He bought the television rights to his sixty-six Hopalong movies, hooked a whole new generation on the hero, and struck pure gold in product endorsements, whereupon he hung up his spurs and retired — out West, of course — in 1953.

DANIEL DECATUR EMMETT

American actors had been appearing in blackface since the Revolution, but it was Mt. Vernon-born Daniel Decatur Emmett who organized the first minstrel show in 1842. His four-man troupe, the Virginia Minstrels, invented a new form of entertainment in New York City when they performed for the first time "an entire evening of oddities, peculiarities, eccentricities, and comicalities of the Sable Genius of Humanity." When Emmett wedded skits and songs to a Black persona, he started an entertainment craze that lasted fifty years, although he is far more famous for writing *Dixie,* the Confederacy's unofficial anthem and one of the nation's favorite tunes. But copyrights being a nebulous concept in the 1800's, the largely unacknowledged Father of the Minstrel Show died poor in Mt. Vernon in 1904. Ironically, this Yankee's musical talent had not only aided the Confederacy but also abetted a pernicious stereotype of Black Americans, which would take the formidable pen of Harriet Beecher Stowe and a century of Supreme Court decisions to dispel.

CLARK GABLE

He had five wives, but a million other women must have been in love with him. Gable could project more masculinity in sixty seconds on the silver screen than a barroom full of steelworkers on a Saturday night. He was a Movie Star, and the secret of his success was his utterly *American* brand of virility — raw, confident, and energetic, just the sort of rough-around-the-edges persona you would expect from a fellow born and raised in the mining town of Cadiz. And though exceedingly handsome, Gable never took himself too seriously. "I'm just a lucky slob from Ohio," said the undis-

"There is no use trying to explain Clark Gable. He simply possessed, through the strange and fantastic medium of the camera, a dynamic and glittering force."
— *Adela Roger St. John, 1932*

puted King of the Box Office. In the 1934 film *It Happened One Night,* his bare chest annihilated undershirt sales across the nation. And five years later, he gave a landmark performance in *Gone With the Wind,* which is probably the nation's favorite film of all time. As the dashing realist Rhett Butler, Gable was the archetype of the lady's man who is also his own man. He died in 1960, leaving behind his only child (a son born posthumously) and his films, which happily, have kept his image forever young.

"Don't you see, I AM Rhett Butler."
— Gable, 1939

LILLIAN GISH
In 1987, when she had completed her 107th film, the producer said of actress Gish, "Inside the lace glove, there's a hand of steel." But only a woman of strength would have climbed onto an ice floe in the teeth of a blizzard and gambled that her celluloid hero would rescue her before she reached the falls. That footage from D.W. Griffith's *Way Down East* became, of course, the definitive scene of silent films, the theatrical touchstone for the twentieth century that Eliza's perils on the Ohio River in *Uncle Tom's Cabin* had been in the nineteenth. At the tail end of that century, Lillian Gish and her sister Dorothy were born in Ohio, where their down-on-her-luck mother put her pretty little girls to work on the popular melodrama circuit. In 1902, Gish made her stage debut on the shoulders of Walter Huston in the tiny Ohio crossroads of Rising Sun. The play was *In Convict's Stripes,* and the six-year-old actress earned ten dollars a week. Director Griffith, who gave the new medium of motion pictures their "form and grammar," needed young faces for work under the harsh lights, and at age thirteen, Gish became a leading lady for filmdom's founding genius. Griffith elevated movies to an art form, and Lillian, with her amazing grace and strength, earned her place as "The First Lady of the Screen" in such classics as *The Birth of a Nation* (1915), the first full-length motion picture. Dozens of roles in the legitimate theater, on Broadway, in the "talkies," and even on television followed. Lillian played Hester Prynne and Camille; she

'I've never known what to do except work; if you start acting when you're five there isn't a lot of point in trying to find something else to do when you're 84. I expect I'll still have a couple of days' shooting to do when they bury me.

Lillian Gish

did comedy and drama, Coward and Chekhov; her 1953 teleplay *The Trip to Bountiful* ended up in the Museum of Modern Art. For more than eight decades now, Gish has practiced her craft, and as one critic noted, "has never failed either the author or the audience."

MARGARET HAMILTON

When she was growing up in Cleveland, her parents wanted her to be a teacher, and Hamilton dutifully attended a kindergarten training school. But the acting bug bit, and she gave up teaching to train at the Cleveland Play House in the late Twenties. A part in a Broadway play led her to Hollywood, where *Another Language* with Helen Hayes started her on a film career that spanned four decades. Because of her strong features, Hamilton was cast as a character actress and in 1939, found the role of a lifetime, the tyrannical Wicked Witch in an American classic, *The Wizard of Oz*. Although the Witch made Judy Garland's Dorothy character shake in her ruby slippers, Hamilton maintained a teacher's interest in children, and she refused to reprise the Witch role for fear it would confuse them. Even in the late 1970's, she was delighted to be receiving (and answering) as many as 2000 letters a year from young fans of Hollywood's most famous witch.

BOB HOPE

"I left England when I was four," Hope once quipped, "because I found out I could never be king." When his stonemason father immigrated to Cleveland, he learned soon enough that America had no kings, so Hope became the nation's court jester instead. His show business career began in Cleveland, his first earnings being the stove that he won for his mother in a Charlie Chaplin impersonation contest. An all-around talent, Hope successfully marched to the tunes of twentieth century's on-going parade of entertainment forms, starring in vaudeville, Broadway, motion pictures, radio, and television. He pioneered the modern monologue, and his rapid-fire delivery — packing a series of topical jokes and one-liners into a few minutes on stage — is still his trademark.

Not only was he one of the first comedians to hire joke writers, but also to admit it. His *Pepsodent Show* on NBC radio in 1938 made Hope's name a household word, but his performances for U.S. servicemen turned him into something of an icon. From World War II through Vietnam, Hope earnestly entertained the troops with troupes of his own, giving the men in uniform a few laughs, a taste of home, and the requisite pretty girls to gape at. Ironically, it was the very unfunny business of war that gave the comedian the international stature to rub elbows with presidents and heads of state. Often called a "compulsive performer," Hope is still working. He certainly does not need the money, but he surely does like the laughs. After seven decades of ham and cheesecake, Hope springs eternal, for which most folks would simply echo his theme song, *Thanks For The Memories*. He may not have had the lightest feet, strongest voice, or handsomest face, but like all great performers, Hope's timing has always been impeccable.

JULIA MARLOWE

One Broadway critic called her "all that is most wholesome and winsome in American womanhood." Quite a review for an actress who lived over a saloon in Portsmouth when she was a little girl and got her start by dancing in local hotels that catered to traveling salesmen. Her big break came in the 1880's when she was a teenager. Colonel Robert Miles, who managed Cincinnati's Grand Opera House spotted Fannie Brough (a.k.a. Sarah Frances Frost) and took her under his wing. Miles engaged the fine English actress Ada Dow as Fannie's tutor, and when life imitated *Pygmalion*, the Shakespearian actress Julia Marlowe was born. Ambitious and attractive enough to still be playing ingenues in her thirties, Marlowe debuted in New York in 1887. Four decades later, she not only appeared in more of Shakespeare's dramas before more people than any other actress in history, but also had accomplished the theatrical first of playing the Bard's work with commercial as well as critical success. Her performances as Juliet in *Romeo and Juliet* became

"Julia Marlowe is a creature apart on the English-speaking stage. There is not a woman player in America or in England that is — attractively considered — fit to unlace her shoe."
— New York Sun, 1903

Marlowe's signature role and made her internationally famous, especially after she married her leading man, E.H. Sothern, in 1911. Such was her artistic prestige that in 1921, George Washington University awarded her the first honorary Doctor of Letters ever bestowed on an American actor.

ANNIE OAKLEY

She was among the first of the superstars. The dark-haired teenager who started out shooting game on her family's Darke County farm ended up, at the turn of the century, as one of the world's most popular and famous performers. For nearly two decades, Annie was a featured sharpshooter in Buffalo Bill Cody's Wild West, an artfully action-packed pageant that created cowboy and Indian adventures for city audiences hungry for a taste of the West's romance. Annie appeared the picture of femininity in her fringed skirts, but when she raised her rifle, she could outshoot any man, including her husband, marksman Frank Butler, whom she met — and bested — at a Cincinnati shooting match in 1875. Butler had the good sense to take a back seat to her talent, and Annie commanded a thousand dollars a week in the Wild West. Her sharpshooting dazzled Queen Victoria (who accurately assessed her as a "very very clever little girl"), and she was even asked to shoot a cigarette from the lips of Kaiser Wilhelm (successfully, thank you). Though "her name was on the lips of every man, woman, and child in America and Europe," it was Sitting Bull who gave Annie her most enduring plaudit, the nickname "Little Miss Sure Shot."

VIRGINIA "MA PERKINS" PAYNE

She was warm and caring and down to earth. And she gave the *best* advice, just like a mother should. Well, certainly she did. She was Ma Perkins, and thousands of people listened to her trials and triumphs on the radio every day. When the *Ma Perkins* program debuted on station WLW in Cincinnati in 1933, it was one of the first radio melodramas. Sponsored by soap company Procter & Gamble, the episodes popularized the term "soap opera," especially

"A soap opera is a kind of sandwich, whose recipe is simple enough, although it took years to compound. Between thick slices of advertising spread twelve minutes of dialogue, add predicament, villainy, and female suffering in equal measure, throw in a dash of nobility, sprinkle with tears, season with organ music, cover with a rich announcer sauce, and serve five times a week."
— James Thurber, 1948

"I guess what I'm talking about is living. Taking the days as they come, the seasons, living for each day itself, just living! Putting up screens in May and taking 'em down in September. Doing your work."

— Ma Perkins

after NBC billed the show as *Oxydol's Own Ma Perkins*. Virginia Payne played the title role for nearly thirty years, a track record equalled by no other radio actress. Listeners from Europe to Hawaii believed her to be a solid senior citizen in the mythical community of Rushville Center, but Payne was actually a much younger — and unmarried — actress in the Queen City. Her identity became so sublimated to Ma Perkins that she stayed out of the public eye until her age caught up with her character's. By 1957, *Time* magazine calculated that Ma's good sense had resolved more than a hundred crises, among them "alcoholism, civic intrigue, and second marriage." But even the wisdom of a maternal Rock of Ages could not compete with television, and on November 25, 1960, *Ma Perkins* signed off for the final time. Ma herself had the last lines: "Goodbye, and may God bless you."

THE WILD MEN OF BORNEO
For fifty years, Hiram and Barney Davis were popular attractions at dime museums and circus sideshows throughout the United States and Europe. They were natural brothers and dwarfs from Knox County, but in the 1850's, a promoter exhibited them as Pluto and Waino, the sons of the emperor of Borneo, a billing which capitalized, literally, on the public's fascination with the nineteenth century's expeditions to exotic lands. Hiram and Barney were retarded, but not nearly so severely as they made the public think they were. And contrary to their manager's very effective publicity, they were neither violent nor uncivilized. Nonetheless, the brothers put on such a good show with their "gibberish and guttural howls" that they earned quite a nice living for themselves. Even in death, they remained inseparable and were buried side by side in a cemetery near their hometown. Though their headstone says simply "Little Men," their lasting legacy is the far more colorful phrase, "The Wild Men of Borneo," which has entered the language as a synonym for boisterous behavior.

"When found they spoke no intelligible tongue and uttered a strange mixture of gibberish and gutteral howls; so wild and ferocious were they that they could easily subdue tigers."
— *Roger Bogdon, Freak Show*

The Wild Men of Borneo
with their guardian, H. A. Warner

■ *Twenty ways in which Ohio invented America, with home-grown ideas and events widely adopted and adapted to become essential ingredients of the nation's style and substance*

SHAKESPEARE IN AMERICA, 1835
Shakespeare in America didn't exist before the 1830's. The founders of New England never thought about him. It was William Holmes McGuffey, the son of Scotch-Irish parents who settled in the forests of Ohio, who brought Shakespeare to America. He created two school readers to be used as basic English textbooks, and Shakespeare was his favorite excerpted author. Shakespeare's popularity then spread to the strolling players who followed flatboats down the rivers. In Florida, for example, in the late 1830's a company put on a performance during the Second Seminole War. The entire company was butchered by the Indians, who looted the costume trunk and galloped off dressed as Orlando, MacBeth, and Othello. Thus Shakespeare, by way of McGuffey, transformed illiterate frontier schoolchildren with fears of Indians, gunfights, and stabbings into literate schoolchildren with fears of ghosts, sleepwalkings, and suffocations.

TEXAS, 1836
With the fall of the Alamo still thundering in their ears, Sam Houston and his small army squared off for yet another battle with Santa Anna on April 21. But this time, the Texans won their independence, defeating the Mexicans in a mere twenty minutes, thanks in no small part to big guns from Cincinnati, a pair of 800-pound cannons known as the Twin Sisters. Ohio's contribution to the cause boomed a new republic into existence, and Texas — and the Texans — have been booming ever since.

AMERICA'S NATURAL SWEET TOOTH, 1851
An eccentric minister in Oxford, Ohio showed the rest of the country how to solve its major beekeeping problem: how to harvest honey without killing bees. Lorenzo Langstroth, after astutely observing the bee's own prefer-

ence for space, developed a rectangular hive with moveable frames, thus inventing the modern beehive. His design was so flawless, it has yet to be changed.

THE CIVIL WAR, 1851

It was in Cincinnati that Harriet Beecher Stowe heard the story that later became the indelible image for slavery and the underground railroad — Eliza crossing the Ohio River ice. *Uncle Tom's Cabin* was quite likely the most morally persuasive American book of the century, and if it was apocryphal that President Lincoln once greeted Mrs. Stowe as "the little woman who wrote the book that started this big war," there was also not much doubt that her book tipped Northern sentiment against slavery and hastened the great civil war.

REALISM IN AMERICAN FICTION, CIRCA 1880

While William Dean Howells, the old Brahmin from Martins Ferry, did not singlehandedly forge the beginnings of Naturalism on American shores, he did forge its definition, calling his theories "the truthful treatment of fiction," a somewhat radical notion for the ornamental Victorian Age. His *A Modern Instance,* for example, was the first American novel to use divorce as a major theme. The definition and defenses of realism in American fiction were major contributions, and Howells became the dean of American letters, as well as the first Ohioan to earn a literary reputation of the first order.

THE MEDIA EVENT, 1881

The high keening of the journalistic pack treeing its quarry has become a staple of contemporary life, and its roots may be traced to the confluence of tragic events over a summer late in the last century, after the new president, Ohioan James Garfield, was shot. His long struggle with death coincided with a revolution in the communications industry — the evolving competencies of telegraphy and printing. Historian Allan Peskin calls this death-watch perhaps the best-known, most closely followed story of the century. At any rate, Garfield's

The reaction to Uncle Tom's Cabin *was — putting it mildly — mixed. Mrs. Stowe received not only an audience with Queen Victoria, but also the ears of a black man in her mail.*

brave struggle became the first such event of modern times. In our times, the brave struggle more often belongs to the beseiged audience.

MODERN SALESMANSHIP, 1885

John H. Patterson, a Dayton toll-collector and coal merchant, bought the patent for the mechanical cash register and set about replacing the one-cent pencil with his $125 machine. To overcome this lapse of economic logic, Patterson hired a sales force, teaching them how to dress and how to make a presentation. His innovations included direct-mail selling and exclusive territories. He is also credited with developing the modern factory, along with most of the practices that distinguish modern American business, even though he sometimes told his men where to buy their neckties and was, in turn, called by one of them "a combination of Julius Caesar and Alice in Wonderland."

THE SIX-PACK, 1886

The Patent Office called the process of making aluminum commercially viable one of the nineteen most important U.S. inventions. It was made possible by the priggish son of a poor Ohio minister, Charles Martin Hall, who discovered the process on a cookstove in an Oberlin woodshed. Hall, a piano-playing liberal arts major, struggled through trial-and-error, fund-raising, and a mountain of litigation to begin Alcoa Aluminum. Thus, that indisputably modern social artifact, the six-pack, had its origin in an Ohio woodshed.

THE THEORY OF RELATIVITY, 1887

Albert Michelson and Edward Morley, two Case Western Reserve professors, with a basement experiment featuring rotating mirrors floating in a tub of mercury, failed in their search for an invisible ether they thought existed to conduct light. But what they *did* do was make astounding measurements accurate to one part in 100 million and lay the foundation upon which Einstein would later build his theory of relativity and our modern theories of time and light. Michelson never gave up on

When a man gets indispensable, let's fire him.

John Henry Patterson

ether, however. When Einstein made his last visit to Michelson in 1931, his daughter asked Einstein, "Please, just don't get him started on the subject of ether."

HOLLYWOOD, 1887
When Daeida Hartell Wilcox heard about an estate called Hollywood, she thought the name would be perfect for a project of hers near her California ranch. Holly trees are not native to the Los Angeles area, but then neither was Mrs. Wilcox, a daughter of Defiance County, who made a capital contribution to motion pictures by founding a new city, which she not only planned and platted but also endowed with land for the first churches, school, library, post office, town hall, police station, and, as befits the climate, tennis court. Mrs. Wilcox never anticipated the glamour that became her city's hallmark, but Tinsel Town sprang, iron-ically, from a woman born in Hicksville.

THE NEW DEAL, 1894
After the 1893 depression, a well-off Massillon quarry owner named Jacob Coxey, a currency reformer and better-roads advocate, devised a plan for federally-supported public improve-ments. His ideas culminated in the famous Coxey's Army, the first protest march on Wash-ington, which tramped from Massillon to peti-tion Congress. The Feds lent a deaf ear, but this was the first attempt at defining joblessness as a national problem that required government intervention. Coxey's march helped chip away at the prevailing notion that unemployment was the result of laziness, and his call for public works jobs anticipated a central element of the 1930's New Deal programs.

"I contend that the only real money is that fiat of the Government. Money is simply an idea that Congress enacted into law. It is represen-tative of value, and should never have a value in and of itself."
— Jacob Coxey

YELLOW JOURNALISM, 1897
When the foreman for the press at the New York *World* needed an illustration to test a new quick-drying yellow ink, Lancaster na-tive Richard Outcault, the paper's cartoonist, drew a series about a gap-toothed, jug-eared munchkin who wore a nightgown. The press-man inked the gown yellow, and the Yellow Kid's subsequent popularity fueled the Hearst-

❝Do not think for a moment that all profiteers and grafters are confined to the Democratic Party.❞

Jacob Coxey

"He is without re-deeming vices, without amiable inconsistencies, without obsessions. He simply does not 'clas-sify.' You cannot ac-curately adjectivize him. He does not defy analysis; he baffles it. It is as if the soul of him, condensed, compressed by environment, or heredity, or some great natural force — not by self-effort — had been molded into a statue, full of vitality, yet im-mobile; a statue with veins . . ."

— financial writer Edwin LeFevre, on Flagler

Pulitzer rivalry, with Outcault bouncing back and forth between the papers. The scenario gave birth to the pejorative description of edi-torial sensationalism we now know as "yellow journalism."

MODERN FLORIDA, CIRCA 1885
Handsome, roguish Henry Flagler and Cleve-land refinery owner John Rockefeller created Standard Oil, quite an achievement in itself. Then Flagler dealt himself out, looked south-ward to the gigantic alligator farm that Florida was at the time, and, unprecedented in the annals of American land development, created out of his own wealth the Florida East Coast railway, which converted Florida from a wil-derness into a twentieth century superstate.

THE ASSEMBLY LINE, CIRCA 1900
Henry Ford II always contended that it was Ohio's Porkopolis — Cincinnati — that gave the world the assembly line. He said his grand-father visited the Queen City at the turn of the century and saw the slaughterhouses with the pigs hung on belts, parts being removed as the carcass traveled along. He thought that if the pig could be disassembled in this manner, then perhaps other things — notably the auto — could be *assembled* in the same manner.

THE POPULARITY OF GOLF, CIRCA 1900
John D. Rockefeller's 700-acre Cleveland estate had a nine-hole golf course where he obsessive-ly played a sport most of America regarded as a preposterous British eccentricity. Newspaper photographers followed him everywhere, and for nearly forty years, the image of Rockefeller on the greensward was a journalistic staple. And so, millions of his fellow Americans, rich and poor, were led, as one historian wrote, "into the same feverish chase." Ohio's revolu-tionary contribution to the game's specifics, however, was the invention of the modern golf ball itself, a ball with a rubber-wound core patented in 1899 by Clevelander Coburn Has-kell. It replaced the universal gutta-percha ball of the day, giving golfers, in the best sense of the word, a better lie.

"I cheat my boys every time I get a chance. I want to make them sharp. I trade with the boys and skin them and just beat them every time I can."
— John D. Rockefeller's father, Big Bill

John D. Rockefeller

THE AMERICAN BUNGALOW, 1902

Two brothers from Cincinnati, Charles and Henry Greene, burst almost overnight out of obscurity and into the annals of architecture with their carefully articulated, wonderfully crafted, original houses that became known as the "California bungalow," but influenced the craft of home-building across the country. Charles, the artist, and Henry, the engineer, complemented each other perfectly in their design, which integrated architecture, native materials, furniture, fixtures, fabric — even landscaping. With them, the Arts and Crafts movement achieved its highest moment.

MODERN COLLEGE GAME, 1913

During a seemingly uneventful summer on the shore of Cedar Point, two young collegians by the names of Gus Dorias and Knute Rockne learned to toss — and catch — the over-inflated lump of leather that then passed for a football. The amusement park was paying them as lifeguards, but in reality, subsidizing a revolutionary development in college athletics. The pair took their new game east to play that Goliath of American football, Army, and with an unforeseen passing game, pasted the troops, 35-13. That summer at Cedar Point established both the forward pass and Notre Dame as a gridiron power. Said Rockne afterward, "We went out like crusaders. We were representing the whole aspiring Midwest."

AMERICAN BEEFCAKE, 1931

Times and manners being what they were, not much happened on the national Cake scene before Johnny Weismuller, noted Olympian, was hired by the Piqua Hosiery Company to pitch Piqua long johns. Piqua, of course, is the birthplace of the drop-seat union suit, another original addition from the heartland to America's *haute couture*. Soon to become filmdom's newest Tarzan, Weismuller traded Piqua for Hollywood and the drop-seat for a loincloth, which prompted perhaps another original: exotic underwear for men.

THE INTEGRATION OF BASEBALL, 1947

It took a disparate set of circumstances to put blacks on America's ball diamond — the life of Branch Rickey and the death of Judge Kenesaw Mountain Landis. Rickey, the son of a fundamentalist Ohio farm couple who didn't allow him to play baseball on Sunday, was the president of the Brooklyn Dodgers, who brought Jackie Robinson into the major leagues. But that didn't occur until the passing of the cantankerous old racist, Landis, another Ohioan, who for nearly 25 years was the most powerful figure in baseball. Rickey said his impulse came from coaching at Ohio Wesleyan, where he watched the pain of his black catcher after being turned away from an Indiana hotel. It was more likely a combination of decency *and* Rickey's business pragmatism: even white folks would one day pay to see blacks play baseball.

THE DONALD TRUMP EGO, CIRCA 1960

According to Donald Trump's autobiography, he and his father, while reading FHA foreclosures, came across Cincinnati's Swifton Village, a troubled 1200-unit apartment development. They put in a minimal bid, and without putting down any of their own money, paid less than $6 million for a project that two years before had cost twice as much. They repaired it, put in good management, then sold it for a $6 million profit. Trump was still in college, and this was his seminal deal. What profiteth a man if he gain Swifton Village and lose any sense of modesty? Plenty.

"Almost everything about Judge Kenesaw Mountain Landis was slightly larger than life, even his name. Before his career was over, it seemed that 'Judge' was his Christian name. With him, reality itself took on slightly askew proportions. Heywood Broun rendered him succinctly in this capsule: 'His career typifies the heights to which dramatic talent may carry a man in America if only he has the foresight not to go on stage.'"

— The Cincinnati Game

■ *A field guide to Ohio, featuring its most sporting fellows, the champions, changers, innovators, pace-setters, and record-breakers who mastered the nation's collegiate and professional games*

PAUL BROWN

When Cleveland's new football franchise held a contest to name the team in 1946, the most popular entry was Browns, a telling tribute to the just-hired coach, whose spectacular records at Ohio State and his hometown high school in Massillon were already rendering him a football icon. Brown's Massillon Tigers took six consecutive state titles and were twice named the nation's scholastic champions, and in 1942, he led OSU to the national collegiate title in only his second year as coach. The magic continued from the 1940's through 1950's, when Cleveland and "the Paul Brown System" dominated pro football with seven national championships. In 1968, Brown started the Cincinnati Bengals, whom he coached until retiring to their front office in 1975. Brown's contributions to the game include the messenger play-call system, face guards on helmets, and putting players in classrooms, where he even graded their playbooks. He crossed pro football's invisible color line by signing blacks in his first Cleveland season, and his "alumni" comprise an all-star cast of the nation's coaches and players. One of football's all-time winningest coaches, Brown remains the only man who (1) took both college and NFL teams to national championships, (2) founded two teams, and (3) has a pro team for a namesake.

WAYNE WOODROW "WOODY" HAYES

A writer once said that Hayes wore a scarlet "O" cap for so many years that it seemed to be part of his head. A most astute observation, considering that before Hayes came to Columbus, Ohio State University was called the graveyard of college football coaches, thanks to the ardent, but acutely fickle, Buckeye fans. Hayes changed all that, lasting through twenty-eight Ohio autumns because he did precisely what the impassioned inhabitants of Ohio Stadium

"The reason I fumbled was because my coach was Woody Hayes. And the reason I picked it up and went for a touchdown was because my coach was Woody Hayes."

— *Johnny Pont, after fumbling the opening kickoff of his first varsity game, then going 96 yards to score*

wanted him to do: win football games. Between 1951 and 1978, Hayes had 205 wins, ten ties, and only 61 losses. He took 13 Big Ten conference titles and 5 national championships, coached 58 All-Americans, and won four Rose Bowls. Often, when a game wasn't going his way, he peeled off his trademark cap and stomped on it. Some said his well-publicized tirades were mere theater. Others saw it as the pure raging of a football perfectionist frustrated by an imperfect world. Though Hayes alternately cuffed his players and mother-henned them, he brought Ohio State football into modern times with his curiously old-fashioned brand of "three yards and a cloud of dust" football. Like his hero, Billy Sherman (known to the rest of the world as General William Tecumseh), Hayes preferred a methodical ground-based attack to the razzle-dazzle of taking to the air. His strategy worked beautifully in the golden years 1968-76, when he lost only thirteen games, and was the big fish in the Big Ten's pond. Hayes became one of the five winningest college coaches in football, which to him was a metaphor for life. "Without winners, there can be no civilization," he wrote. But in his zeal to win, Hayes's behavior became uncivilized, and finally, he slugged — on television for all the world to see — a Clemson player during the 1978 Gator Bowl. Hayes was never bitter about his firing, although his wish to die on the 50-yard line would never come true. In Columbus, he came to be regarded with the gentle affection reserved for patriarchs, and when he died in 1987, flags flew at half-staff across the city. "If Woody isn't a legend," said one cohort, "he'll do until one comes along."

JOHN HEISMAN

Born in Cleveland in 1869, Heisman was a pioneer of modern football. He lobbied for game quarters and the forward pass, taught teams to start plays with voice signals, invented the snap from center, and developed the "Heisman shift," the granddaddy of the I and T formations. Heisman was "a natural" who earned one of the first football letters at Penn, but he

"A prolate spheroid in which the outer leather casing is drawn tightly over a somewhat smaller rubber tubing."
— John Heisman's definition of a football

cut his coaching teeth at Oberlin College, where his undefeated 1892 season was the springboard for a career that took him to schools from Texas to Pennsylvania. A trained actor, Heisman often sowed flowery phrases on the field of play, but his pretty words never belied his aggressive winning style. In his handbook, *The Principles of Football,* he wrote, "(A coach) has no time to say 'please' or 'mister,' and he must be occasionally severe, arbitrary, and something of a czar." The Heisman Trophy, awarded annually to the best college football player, is named in his honor.

JACK NICKLAUS

When he won the U.S. Open in 1962, Nicklaus was only 22, the youngest golf champion in nearly four decades. They put his picture on the cover of *TIME*. Not bad for a kid from Columbus, the blond, burly "Golden Bear," who with the dew from the links at Ohio State still fresh on his clubs, toppled America's golf king, the venerable Palmer, and sent "Arnie's Army" into retreat. With his concentration and powerful swing, Nicklaus dominated golf for a quarter of a century. A multi-time PGA Player of the Year, he is the only man to win the five major tournaments — U.S. Open, Masters, PGA, U.S. Amateur, British Open — *twice,* and his career earnings exceed $5 million. But his most impressive record, and a telling measure of his greatness, is his endurance. When he won the U.S. Masters in 1986, he was 46, the oldest champion of any decade, and his win put the incomparable Nicklaus signature on the mantle of Time.

JESSE OWENS

He was the toast of the 1936 Berlin Olympics, but Owens' dash to fame began at a Cleveland junior high school, where even then his untrained legs took him 100 yards in a record ten seconds. Owens' given name was James Cleveland, but Records *should* have been his middle one, because setting new marks in track and field was his specialty. In high school, he owned three — 100-yard dash, 220-yard dash, and broad jump — and in 1935, wearing the

"Jesse Owens didn't run, he floated. He was the prettiest runner I ever saw."

— *Arthur Daley,*
New York Times

Scarlet and Gray of Ohio State at a track meet in Ann Arbor, he became the only person to ever establish six records in one day, a feat made all the more remarkable because Owens achieved them in only 45 minutes. But if Michigan was a piece of cake for him, then Berlin provided the frosting. Owens took four gold medals — 100-meter dash, 200-meter dash, 400-meter relay, and broad jump — and his shining victory was moral as well as athletic. He, a black American, had with enormous dignity and grace stolen the Olympics out from under the racist nose of Adolph Hitler.

BRANCH RICKEY

They called him "Mr. Baseball" and "The Mahatma." The accolades stemmed from Rickey's talent for finding and developing good ball players, and this was the particular genius with which he founded three baseball dynasties. Rickey was born in 1881, in the hardscrabble southern Ohio hill country to a farm couple who eventually moved to Lucasville so that their bright boy could enjoy the advantages of a town school. From his athletic father, Rickey inherited the genes that put him on the Ohio Wesleyan baseball team, and from his Scripture-reading mother, he got the philosophy that kept him off the diamond on Sundays. When tuberculosis interrupted his playing career, and hard times undermined his law practice, Rickey turned to major league baseball, becoming a scout, manager, and finally executive. Players knew him as shrewd and something of a skinflint, but if Rickey ran his teams with an iron hand in a leather glove, he was also considered humane and impeccably fair-minded. His leadership of the St. Louis Cardinals (1917-1942), Brooklyn Dodgers (1942-1950), and Pittsburgh Pirates (1950-1960) made powerhouses and pennant winners of them all. Along the way, Rickey signed more than a few baseball greats — Campanella, Clemente, Newcombe; and he made two contributions that changed the game forever — the farm team in 1919, and racial integration in 1947. Rickey broke major league baseball's long ban on black players by signing Jackie

"Rose is a hanging curveball that history has served up right in front of our eyes. In the tobacco-stained archive reserved for baseball, he has been a revolving centerpiece, streaking before us in all of his naked determination. Rose is the bridge between the Cobb and the Max Headroom generations, a switch-hitting metaphor who embodied the old ballplaying ways and the newest means, a player for both McGraw and NBC."

— The Cincinnati Game

Robinson to the Dodgers. His famous decision not only strengthened baseball, but also, ultimately, the country by calling attention to the national hypocrisy about civil rights. It is said that Rickey waited forty years to find the right man with the intelligence and moral courage to successfully integrate baseball. The virtue of Rickey's patience was no less than could be expected from someone who called the notebook where he tracked potential players, the "Bible."

PETE ROSE

His pinnacle came in Cincinnati on September 11, 1985, when Rose, on the fifty-seventh anniversary of Ty Cobb's last baseball game, surpassed said Mr. Cobb's 4,191 base hits, the record that conventional sports wisdom said could never be broken. Rose — in his hometown, at the overripe age of 44, playing for the Reds with whom his major league career began twenty-three years before — had defied the odds, thus elevating himself to the small pantheon of baseball dieties. Years before, no less than the mythic Mickey Mantle had pegged Rose as "Charlie Hustle," an acutely apt sobriquet for a man who overcompensated for his lack of "natural ability" with a sheer, unabashed love of the game. Whatever the thorns in his personal life, Rose wore both his heart and soul on his uniform sleeve, and his phenomenal desire to play carried him to giddy status in the litany of baseball mosts — hits, at bats, games, winning games, singles, seasons with 200 or more hits. And he is the only man in baseball to have played 500 games at five positions — first, second, and third base, left and right field. Rose the Player yielded to Rose the Manager in 1986, but not before he had tacked another 64 base hits onto his record, ensuring a long haul for any would-be equal of this perpetual Boy of Summer.

DENTON "CY" YOUNG

As a young man, he could throw a baseball so hard that it reminded folks of a cyclone, and thus "Cy" Young found his nickname and began carving out his incomparable place on the mound in the Ohio towns near his Tuscarawas County farm. He began his major league career with the Cleveland Spiders in 1890, pitching (and winning) in his first season a double-header that signaled the greatness yet to come. He played in the first forerunner of the World Series (1903; his Boston Red Sox won); pitched three no-hit, no-run games and the first perfect game (1904); and until 1968, held the record for the most games pitched (906). Though Young quit in 1911, three of his lifetime records still stand: most wins (511), completed games (751), and innings pitched (7377), and he remains the only pitcher to win 200 games in both leagues. He was, of course, a shoo-in for the Baseball Hall of Fame, and the annual Cy Young Award, given to baseball's best pitcher, fittingly bears the name of the Ohioan who set the pace for generations of pitchers. Young spent most of his major league career in Cleveland, and upon retiring his splendid arm, he returned home to a Tuscarawas County farm.

STALWART OHIO FIRSTS

Johnny Vander Meer, *Cincinnati Reds*
First and only major league pitcher with back-to-back no-hitters, against Braves and Dodgers, June 11 and 15, 1938

Joe Nuxhall, *Cincinnati Reds*
Twentieth century's youngest major league baseball player, age 15, 1944

Neal Ball, *Cleveland Indians*
Made first unassisted triple play in major leagues, July 19, 1909

Bill Wambsganss, *Cleveland Indians*
Made first unassisted triple play in World Series, October 10, 1920

Les Horvath, *Ohio State*
First and only Big Ten quarterback to win the Heisman Trophy, 1944

"Sure, I know I make more money than the president of the United States. But he can't hit a slider."
— *Pete Rose*

Louis Sockalexis, *Cleveland Spiders*
First American Indian to play major league baseball, 1897-99

Charles Follis, *Wooster*
First black professional football player, Shelby (Ohio) Blues, 1904-06

Moses and Welday Walker, *Mt. Pleasant*
First black players in major league baseball, Toledo, 1884

Frank Robinson, *Cleveland Indians*
First black major league manager, 1975

Ray Chapman, *Cleveland Indians*
First and only major league player killed by a pitched ball (thrown by the Yankee's Carl Mays), August 16, 1920

William DeHart Hubbard, *Cleveland*
First black American to win an Olympic Gold Medal (broad jump, 24 feet, 5¹/₈ inches), 1924

Marge Schott, *Cincinnati*
First woman to purchase a major league sports team, the Cincinnati Reds, 1984

Archie Griffin, *Ohio State University*
First and only college football player to win Heisman Trophy in consecutive years, 1974-75

Ohio State football team
First Big Ten school to play in all major Bowl games — Rose, Orange, Cotton, Sugar, Fiesta, 1921-1987

First NFL Playoff Game
Chicago Bears – 9, Portsmouth Spartans – 0, December 18, 1932

William Howard Taft, *President, United States of America*
Having warmed-up during his Cincin-

NFL Midwives: teams present at birth of pro football in Canton, 1920
Canton Bulldogs
Akron Pros
Massillon Tigers
Cleveland Indians
Dayton Triangles
Decatur Staleys
Hammond Pros
Rochester Jeffersons
Rock Island
Independents
Muncie Flyers
Racine Cardinals

nati youth as a sandlot catcher, he started the baseball tradition of the President tossing out the season's first ball, doing the honors for the Washington Senators, April 14, 1910

Monday Night Football

To the delight of die-hard fans and the chagrin of their spouses, Cleveland Browns' president Art Modell teamed up with network TV to host the first Monday matchup, the Browns tuning out the Jets 31-21, on September 21, 1970.

Professional baseball

The Cincinnati Baseball Club, a.k.a. Red Stockings, became in 1869, the first all-paid touring team. Though their record — 64 wins, no losses, one tie — was spectacular, their net profit — $1.39 — was not.

Night Baseball

Cincinnati manager Larry McPhail, the "Barnum of Baseball," not only put the Reds under the lights but also got President Roosevelt to throw the switch for the first major league night game, May 24, 1935

NCAA Basketball Tournament

The event began in 1939, at the suggestion of Ohio State basketball coach Harold Olsen, who also chaired the early committees of the tournament that has become the Super Bowl of college basketball.

Penalty Flags

In 1941, Youngstown College football coach Dike Beede provided flags to referees as a substitute for their confusing horns and whistles. One referee, Jack McPhee, used his flag in an Ohio State-Iowa game in Columbus, where the Big Ten commissioner liked what he saw so much that the conference immediately adopted the idea, thus triggering a silent revolution in football.

"Before he left Columbus to become president of the Reds, Larry MacPhail dressed so grandly one writer called him 'a municipal eyesore.' He was otherwise loud, as well, described as having a 'vibrant moose voice.' His biographer states that he was first to introduce organ music to baseball, at Ebbets Field. It was probably the only instrument that could match him in range and volume."

— The Cincinnati Game

■ **FOUNDERS**
Ohioans with good ideas and the best of institutions

▶ To be a Founder is to be part of a rare, but anonymous, population. Founding things is an American preoccupation, a precedent begun in that decade after the Revolution when we former colonials were busy setting up a nation. But as important as that task was, the individuals who accomplished it have become muddled in history, and so we conveniently lump them together as Founding Fathers, a laudatory convention that assures them our proper respect, if not precise recollection.

The Founders that we present here started nothing so important as a nation, but their small notions helped shape the nation. They are Ohioans who instigated movements and organizations that have become American institutions. Though largely little known nor long remembered, they are in their own right, Founding Fathers, individuals whose efforts made a truly lasting impression.

Alcoholics Anonymous — in 1935, William Wilson, a down-on-his-luck stockbroker, helped physician Bob Smith sober up, and soon they were rescuing other alcoholics in "Dr. Bob's" home in Akron, developing treatment methods that are the mainstay of this international organization.

The Boy Scouts of America — Cincinnati-born Daniel Carter Beard wrote a slew of field and forest handbooks for boys, but his lasting contribution to the nation's youth was translating an English idea into the organization that became the Boy Scouts of America in 1910.

U.S. Civil Service — George Pendleton, a Senator from Cincinnati, is best-remembered for sponsoring the Pendleton Act, the landmark 1883 law that established the Civil Service Commission and changed the federal hiring system from spoils to merit.

Women's Christian Temperance Union — in 1873, a preacher inspired women in Hillsboro to "pray and sing the saloons out of business." Their crusade caught on, and in 1874, national delegates met in Cleveland to organize what

"These fools have built an immense city without any place for the young people at all."
— Daniel Carter Beard in New York City

would become a formidable political force, the WCTU.

American Jewish Reform — from his Cincinnati synagogue, Rabbi Issac Mayer Wise launched in the late nineteenth century a national religious movement with a singularly infectious idea: Judaism in the United States should be tailored to American tastes and traditions.

4-H Clubs — in 1902, Springfield Township school superintendent A.B. Graham organized a Boys' and Girls' Agricultural Club to improve rural life with "hands-on" education. The successful program he planted in Clark County bore fruit as the uniquely American 4-H Clubs.

U.S. Weather Bureau — Cleveland Abbe used telegraphed weather data to make daily prognostications for Cincinnati. He convinced the government that nationwide forecasts had merit, and in 1870, President Grant created the U.S. weather bureau, of which "Old Probabilities" Abbe became the first chief.

Weekly Reader — the first issue rolled off the presses in Columbus and into America's classrooms in 1928. Eleanor Johnson started the weekly to bring world news and views to an elementary level, and the newspaper now reaches three-fourths of the nation's schools.

Disabled American Veterans — in 1919, servicemen incapacitated by the Great War met in the Cincinnati home of Judge Robert Marx, who helped them formally organize. After Congress chartered the DAV in 1932, the Cincinnatians became Chapter No. 1, and Marx the first U.S. commander.

The Chautauqua Movement — Akron industrialist Lewis Miller and Methodist minister John Vincent offered classes to Sunday School teachers at Lake Chautauqua in the 1870's. Their self-improvement program started both a national movement and the first organized adult education in the U.S.

■ THE BLUE OHIO YONDER

■ *Magnificient men and their flying machines, Ohioans who put wings on man and man on the moon, giving the world the science, sport, and industry of aviation*

▶ In 1903, the Wright Brothers' heavier-than-air machine took men into the sky. In 1969, Neil Armstrong took them to the moon. Both landmark events were the fantastic technical achievements of Ohioans, men who from the cosmic perspective of space were next door neighbors, the Wrights being from Dayton and Armstrong from Wapakoneta, a mere hundred miles to the north. Only sixty-six years separated the Wrights' airplane from Armstrong's moon walk, barely a lifetime. Yet in that veritable blink of time, aviation soared from air to space.

No place on earth aided and abetted this technological revolution more than Ohio. In the early days of flight, Dayton, predictably, was a center of aviation innovation, and since the Wrights perfected flying there, virtually everything the Brothers did in the air was a first or a record. Yet across the state and throughout the decades, Ohioans have maintained the tradition of being ready and willing pioneers as aviation exploded from a lonely experiment by two methodical men to a full-blown industry. In the process, some Ohioans — Rickenbacker, Glenn, Resnik — have become heroes, while others have been lost in the fast shuffle of modern times. Nonetheless, Ohio remains in the forefront of aerospace research and development and maintains the track record of producing everything from engines to astronauts, more, in fact, of those intrepid travelers than any other state.

The Wright Brothers were turn-of-the-century bicycle mechanics who came up with an incredible sideline that forever altered our concepts of time and space. In 1961, on the edge of the Wright's hometown, the U.S. Air Force officially organized a vast technological complex to design, develop and buy airplanes. Aeronautical Systems Division at Wright-Patterson Air Force Base is now the largest military aviation research and development center in the world, but the airplane's unlikely roots are acknowledged there by the legion of scientists and engineers who — with a respectful nod to the inventive Brothers — simply call their sophisticated workplace the "Bicycle Shop."

1900-1909

1901 — Nation's first wind tunnel built by Wright Brothers for flight experiments in Dayton

1903 — World's first powered flight, made by Orville at windy Kitty Hawk, North Carolina

■ *Wrights have gone 600 miles for airplane ride that lasts twelve seconds; portends today's travel conundrum: trip to airport takes longer than flight*

1905 — First published account of Wrights' flight, in the unlikely journal, *Gleanings in Bee Culture*, by Medina apiarist A.I. Root

"*He flew 67 minutes in a 16-mile wind, handled his pair of planes like a chauffeur, and rode the air as deliberately as if he were passing over a solid macadam road.*"
— *eyewitness account of Orville Wright's 1908 flying demonstration at Ft. Myer*

Wilbur and Orville Wright

■ *Wright Brothers run out of gas during Dayton test flights, execute first fuel emergency landing*

1908 — First person dies in an airplane crash; Flyer propeller cracks, Army Lt. Thomas Selfridge killed, Orville breaks leg

1909 — Orville makes first city-to-city flight, Fort Myer to Alexandria, Virginia; thereby sets new world distance (10 miles), speed (42 mph), and altitude (400 feet) records

Inauspicious boost to military-industrial complex: military aviation is born; U.S. Army has no pilots, but agrees to buy its first airplane from Wrights for $30,000

■ *Katharine Wright ties down her petticoats for a sisterly flight over France, starts hobble skirt fad*

1910-1919

1910 — First flight over water; Glenn Curtiss collects $5000 prize for hop from Euclid Beach to Cedar Point across Lake Erie

First cargo flight; pilot Philip Parmalee takes a bolt of silk from Dayton to Columbus

■ *Orville Wright gives Parmalee a sack lunch, first inflight meal*

1911 — First man to fly over the Rocky Mountains, daring Cromwell Dixon of Columbus conquers the peaks, collects $10,000 prize, dies two days later in plane crash

■ *Post office nixes airmail proposal of Urbana pilot C.P. Wanzer, declares planes unsafe for U.S. Mail*

1917 — First aviation research and development center, McCook Field, Dayton, named for Ohio's Civil War-era family of "Fighting McCooks"

1918 — America's Ace of Aces and national hero in World War I is Eddie Rickenbacker of Columbus, who shoots down 26 enemy aircraft and wins Congressional Medal of Honor

First commercially successful airplane; the Martin MB, nation's first bomber and "probably the finest combat plane designed in the United States," is built by Glenn Martin, Cleveland

1919 — Floyd Smith invents the modern rip-cord parachute in Dayton

■ *Lt. Harold Harris's happy landing in Dayton grape arbor is world's first emergency parachute jump*

First transcontinental air mail flight, Cleveland to Chicago

1920-1929

1923 — Dayton-based Lieutenants John Macready and Oakley Kelly make first nonstop transcontinental flight in Fokker T-2; New York to San Francisco in 26 hours, 50 minutes

1927 — First airport control tower, Cleveland

Eddie Rickenbacker

- *City employees later learn to use radios, become first licensed air traffic controllers*

1929 — First National Air Race, major competition for both men and women pilots, held at Cleveland Municipal Airport

First automatic pilot, Cleveland

1930-1939

1932 — Jimmy Doolittle in fast, but dangerous Gee Bee R-1 sets world speed record: 252.68 mph at National Air Races, Cleveland

First woman to head a municipal airport, Lauretta Schimmoler, in Bucyrus

1933 — First pressure flight suit, designed by B.F. Goodrich's Russell Colley, Akron

1935 — First man to fly over both poles, Hudson's Lincoln Ellsworth; later explores Antarctica, names huge chunk of the continent for his father: Ellsworth Land

1937 — First automatic landing system, in Fokker C-14B, Patterson Field, Dayton

1940-1949

1945 — World War II Ohio ace, Capt. Don Gentile of Piqua downs thirty German planes

1946 — First person to eject from airplane, Sgt. Larry Lambert of Wright Field, Dayton

- *Eddie Rickenbacker ejects the ashes of his pal Damon Runyon over Manhattan*

1948 — The Passing of the Torch; Orville Wright dies, Wapakoneta's Neil Armstrong turns 18

- *Armstrong sets priorities, learns to fly before he learns to drive*

U.S. Air Force combines Dayton's Wright and Patterson Fields; creates Wright-Patterson Air Force Base, a research and development goliath

- *Wright-Patterson AFB builds world's longest runway — 10,000 feet*

1950-1959

1952 — First helicopter crosses Atlantic; pilots of Sikorsky H-19s are Harry Jeffers, Newark, and Harold Moore, Cincinnati

1957 — First man to fly over U.S. at supersonic speed, Marine Lt. Colonel John Glenn of New Concord

- *Glenn sets transcontinental speed record, but bombs over his home town, where folks mistake his F8U Crusader's sonic boom for Armageddon*

1958 — First NASA chief is Cleveland's T. Keith Glennan, the Case Institute of Technology president who guides America's first steps into space

"Neil Armstrong, the first man ever to stand alone on a celestial body, likened the experience to that of a man who, for a moment, is allowed to stand above the crowd, and find enlightenment. Back in the crowd, down from the mountain, his voice becomes one of the many, and is lost in the babble. It is easy to imagine an elderly Columbus, keeping his own counsel, his knotty hands still strong, mending sails."

— Robert McKay,
Ohio Magazine

Neil Armstrong, Jr.

1960-1969

1960 — Alice King Chatham, a Dayton sculptor, custom designs space helmets for Project Mercury astronauts

1961 — Akron's Russell Colley, "Father of Space Suit," designs first ones for U.S. astronauts

1962 — First American in earth orbit, John Glenn

■ *Welcome Home parade in New York sets tickertape record*

1964 — First woman to solo an airplane around the world, Columbus's Jerrie Mock

1965 —· World's first spacecraft rendezvous: Gemini 7 and 6A in tandem orbit; Cleveland native James Lovell is Gemini 7 co-pilot

1966 — Gemini 12 mission gives astronaut Lovell world record for miles spent in earth orbit, seven million

1968 — First manned lunar orbit, Apollo 8 command module pilot is astronaut Lovell

1969 — First man on moon, Apollo 11 Commander Neil Armstrong, whose size 9½ left foot puts first mark of man on the virgin lunar dust

■ *U.S. Playing Card, Cincinnati, deals astronauts a cool hand, manufactures fireproof decks for Apollo missions*

1970-1979

1972 — World's most advanced fighter plane, F-15 Eagle, flies for first time; program is headquartered at Wright-Patterson AFB

1980's

1982 — New generation of U.S. bombers, the B1B; program headquartered at Wright-Patterson AFB; General Electric, Cincinnati, will build engines

1984 — Nation's largest International Airshow and Trade Exposition, annual Dayton event

1985 — World's largest landing gear manufacturer; Cleveland Pneumatic Tool Company

1986 — Space shuttle *Challenger* explodes; Judith Resnik of Akron, member of nation's first class of women astronauts, dies

■ *Nation's oldest civilian parachute school, Greene County Skydiving Center, Xenia*

1987 — B1B, powered by GE F-101 engines, breaks bomber records: speed (669.52 mph), distance (3000 kilometers), payload (66,140 pounds)

1989 — Wright-Patterson is nation's largest U.S. Air Force base with 35,000 personnel and $841 million payroll

■ *Largest privately owned airport in U.S., Airborne Express, Wilmington*

"In the student center at Muskingum, a student who had been in the Marine Corps watched the ascent on television and, in a grand patriotic display, leapt from table to table singing the Marine Corps hymn. He did not sing very well, but he sang vigorously.

Everywhere in the village there was an insurgence of good feeling and patriotism. It was a village of immigrants, after all, and the plumber's son was the newest immigrant, on the primitive frontier of space."

— John Baskin, on John Glenn

John Glenn

■ THE LINCOLN CONNECTION

■ *The complex and star-crossed relationship of ironies, incidents, coincidence, accidents, anecdotes, historical twists, and unexpected, but eventful turns involving Ohio and Abraham Lincoln*

▶ Ohio is connected to Abraham Lincoln in a circumstantial web of love and hate, bitter war and uneasy peace, great issues and small ironies. On the one hand, no state provided more volunteers more quickly than Ohio to help settle the great family feud that fell into Mr. Lincoln's lap; on the other, no state gave him a more vociferous and dangerous critic than the one Ohio produced in the person of Clement Vallandigham.

Conflict was the essence of Lincoln's time in office, and the dissensions of the nation — politics and passion, States' Rights and Slavery, Secession and Union — played themselves out in Ohio. The state became a House Divided, and from the troubled Buckeye soil emerged leading statesmen, great generals, simple soldiers, widows, opportunists, and common folk caught in the cross-fire of competing philosophies. Some of them had a national impact. Most simply hoped to stay out of harm's way until the storm of Secession had passed. And many crossed paths with Lincoln, tied by the strands of history and fate to the Great Emancipator, the Savior of the Union who bound the wounds when politics failed and blood flowed North and South.

MAJOR CHARACTERS

Abraham Lincoln
President of the United States, 1861-1865
A self-schooled lawyer, he guided the nation through the Civil War, the nation's most precarious hour, with single-minded devotion to his paramount goal of preserving the Union. To that end, he issued the Emancipation Proclamation, personally directed a military ill-prepared for war, and with splendid wit and measured wisdom, reassured the people that sacrificing their sons to bring the South back into the nation's fold was not in vain. Five days after Lee surrendered to Grant in April, 1865, Lincoln was assassinated by John Wilkes Booth, a Confederate sympathizer, while attending a play at Ford's Theatre, Washington, D.C.

Cabinet picks

Salmon P. Chase
Secretary of the Treasury
A Cincinnati Abolitionist and Senator from Ohio, he had rivaled Lincoln for the Republican Presidential nomination but served him admirably, not only organizing a national bank in the midst of war, but also inspiring public confidence in it.

Edwin M. Stanton
Secretary of War
When the Steubenville-born attorney first met Lincoln in Cincinnati, he insulted him personally and professionally, but Stanton was a ruthlessly able and incorruptible administrator, which were critical skills for a war-time post.

Salmon P. Chase

"*I beg to present to you as a Christmas gift the city of Savannah.*"
— *Sherman dispatch to Lincoln, 1864*

William Tecumseh Sherman

Lincoln, with malice toward none and charity toward Stanton, gave him the appointment.

William Dennison
Postmaster General

Born in Cincinnati, a man of means and manners, he chaired the 1864 Republican Convention that renominated Lincoln, and as Governor of Ohio, pushed McClellan into Virginia to protect Unionists with Ohio militia, thereby putting what is now West Virginia in the North's hip pocket. In reward, Lincoln put him in charge of the Post Office.

Top kicks

General Ulysses S. Grant

He was the son of a Brown County tanner, a country boy who reluctantly went off to West Point, a failure at the business of civilian life, a tenacious bulldog of a man who did two things really well — ride horses and win battles. That was enough. Lincoln made "Unconditional Surrender" Grant commander of the Union armies in 1864.

General William Tecumseh Sherman

If Grant was Lincoln's right arm, then Sherman was his left. Lancaster-born Sherman proved himself at Bull Run, then in 1864, he trampled his way across Georgia to sack and burn Atlanta. Sherman rewrote the rules of warfare on that famous March to the Sea, and afterwards, the throttled South would not, could not, rise again.

General George B. McClellan

Just months after his western Virginia mission put him in the national spotlight, the young Ohio Captain found himself a general heading the Union Army. But McClellan never failed to hesitate when other officers would act, and Lincoln axed him. With an advanced case of sour grapes, the general paradoxically ran for President on a peace plank, teaming up against his Commander-in-Chief with fellow Cincinnatian George Pendleton as running mate.

General Phil Sheridan

Back home in Perry County, he was always "Little Phil," but he never stood taller than at the Battle of Cedar Creek, prodding the Union lines from a rout to a rally on the famed horseback ride that made him a national hero. "Sheridan's Ride" secured not only the Shenandoah Valley, but also Lincoln's re-election, a double victory that silenced "peace-at-any-price" McClellan by a half million votes.

All the President's men

William Dean Howells

When the Republicans nominated Lincoln in 1860, the young writer from Martins Ferry was asked to pen his official campaign biography, which Howells produced in a week, earning Lincoln's gratitude and appointment as consul to Venice.

John Hay

Lincoln's private secretary married a Cleveland socialite and lived in Ohio thirteen years. Co-author of the massive biography *Abraham Lincoln: A History,* he became Secretary of State under McKinley and Roosevelt and authored the Open Door policy.

Jay Cooke
The Sandusky-born banker helped finance the Civil War for the North. Early in the war, a debt overload threatened to sink Lincoln's ship of state, but Cooke's plan to sell government bonds via commission salesmen raised more than $500 million by 1864.

John Brough
The 1863 Ohio gubernatorial contest was the North's political arm-wrestling in microcosm: hard-biting Copperheads vs. steadfast Unionists, Clement Vallandigham vs. John Brough. The eyes of the nation were on Ohio on election night. When Brough told Lincoln that he won, the President telegraphed back: "Glory to God in the highest. Ohio has saved the Nation."

MINOR PLAYERS

Nicholas Longworth
Cincinnati's first millionaire, Longworth was also the nation's first commercial vintner and a first-class botanist. His celebrated garden attracted visitors, including Lincoln, who in 1855 found the old man weeding and mistook him for the hired help.

Thomas Edison
He was a seventeen-year-old student in Cincinnati with a night job as a telegraph operator. At 3 a.m. on April 15, Edison took the message that shocked the city: the President was dead.

Junius Brutus Booth, Jr.
A professional actor and the brother of John Wilkes Booth, he was appearing at Pike's Opera House in Cincinnati when the President was shot, and hearing the news, fainted. He quietly left town, as Pike's was draped in black for Cincinnati's memorial service to Lincoln.

Thaddeus Lowe
In April, 1861, the aeronaut tried to prove the military value of balloons, taking off from Cincinnati but landing unhappily in South Carolina, where he talked his way out of spy charges. Two months later, he sent the first ground-to-air telegraph message to Lincoln, who authorized a balloon corps with Lowe in charge.

D.K. Cartter
Chairman of the Ohio delegation at the 1860 Republican convention, he switched Ohio's votes from Chase and delivered the party's nomination to Lincoln, who later made him minister to Bolivia.

The Lawrence
The gavel at the 1860 Convention was made of wood from the vessel, Perry's flagship at the Battle of Lake Erie, prompting its president to quip . . . "the auguries are that we shall meet the enemy and they shall be ours."

Daniel Decatur Emmett
In composing "Dixie," the Mt. Vernon native gave the South its unofficial anthem. Ironically, the song was both played at Jefferson Davis's inauguration and requested

Thomas Edison

" *Vallandigham died with his armor on, and it clanged as he fell.*"
— *General McCook*

Clement Vallandigham

by Lincoln at the post-Appomattox celebrations.

Charles Cardwell McCabe
McCabe, a Methodist Episcopal bishop, popularized "The Battle Hymn of the Republic" by teaching it to the Ohio Volunteers and war prisoners. The Athens native sang the anthem for Lincoln, who cried and requested, "Sing it again."

Ohio's Union Light Guard
Ohio Governor David Tod in 1863 selected one hundred sturdy specimens of Buckeye manhood to serve as the President's bodyguards. Since Lincoln often balked at being under the protection, only a skeleton detail was on duty when he was killed.

Bishop Matthew Simpson
The Cadiz native, a Methodist Episcopal minister and Lincoln's favorite speaker, gave the President's funeral oration in Illinois.

Hiram Cook
A member of the Ohio Union Light Guard, this bugler from Circleville sounded "Taps" over the body of Lincoln as the funeral train left Washington.

John A. Bingham
Cadiz's "silver-tongued orator," a lawyer and Congressman and later U.S. Minister to Japan, was the primary prosecutor at the trial of the assassination conspirators.

Thomas Ewing, Jr.
The Union General and lawyer from Lancaster defended Dr. Samuel Mudd and Edward Spangler,

unsuccessfully, at the trial of the assassination conspirators.

THE DISLOYAL OPPOSITION

Clement L. Vallandigham
Lincoln had no bigger thorn in his side than the Congressman from Dayton who led the "Copperheads," Northerners who opposed the Civil War. The vocal Vallandigham grew politically powerful and pushed for overthrowing the Government, whereupon Lincoln had him arrested for "disloyal statements and opinions." Vallandigham cried violation of Free Speech, and with riots occurring over his arrest, was well on his way to becoming a martyr. But Lincoln took the sails out of his wind by shrewdly commuting his sentence to exile in the South. Thus, the first American deported for treasonous activity became the model for *The Man Without A Country,* a country to which he tried returning via the ballot box, running *in absentia* for Governor of Ohio from Canada. Vallandigham lost, and after Appomattox took away his soapbox, the "most unpopular man in the North" returned to practicing law in Dayton.

WITS

Artemus Ward
Lincoln thought him a knee-slapper and often read his columns to friends. Ward, a.k.a. Charles Farrar Browne, became the "Father of American Humor" at the Cleveland *Plain Dealer* with a folksy, "horse laugh" style. In 1862, the President narrated a

Ward story to his bemused Cabinet, providing comic relief before the serious star attraction, his presentation of the Emancipation Proclamation.

Petroleum Vesuvius Nasby

Lincoln not only read aloud the enormously popular Nasby Letters, he *memorized* them. Nasby was the satiric straw man of a Findlay newspaper editor, David Ross Locke. He created the ignorant, hypocritical Copperhead preacher to parody, and thus undermine, the Southern cause. Three things, said one Congressman, had saved the Union: the army, the navy, and the *Nasby Papers.*

October, 1862

During a Cabinet meeting, Postmaster General Dennison noticed the worn leather chair at Lincoln's desk. "I should think," he offered, "that the Presidential chair should be better furniture than that."

Replied Lincoln, "You think that chair is not good, Governor. There are many people who want to sit in it, and I've often wished some of them had it instead of me."

SAYINGS

Now He Belongs to the Ages

With his rudeness turned to respect, Stanton after Ford's Theatre kept a tearful death watch, uttering the precis that now belongs to history and is the only epitaph on Lincoln's tomb.

Don't swap horses in the middle of the stream

Lincoln, to sway voters from McClellan during his 1864 election campaign, told an equine anecdote, and his punchline evolved into a new American maxim.

In God We Trust

In response to public sentiment during the Civil War for official appeal to Higher Authority, Chase literally coined a phrase, putting the words on a two-cent piece in 1864.

His Name is Mudd

Dr. Samuel Mudd, the Maryland physician who innocently treated the broken leg of John Wilkes Booth, was unjustly tried as an assassination conspirator. Tom Ewing's defense of the doctor was splendid, but hopeless against the storm of public fury, and thus from Mudd's conviction came the phrase that still holds his name in contempt.

LINCOLN COUNTRY

Mansfield

In 1858, a Sandusky newspaper reported that at a Mansfield rally, Abraham Lincoln had received his first endorsement for President. The story was picked up by the New York *Herald* and spread to newspapers across the country. In fact, the whole thing was a hoax; the rally and "nomination" never happened. Some think the story was a lark born in the silly pen of David Ross Locke; others say it was planted by a politician to undermine Chase. In any event, people *believed* that Mansfield nominated Lincoln, and the bogus event plucked him out of the political backwater and into the national spotlight.

Dayton

In September, 1859, after his debates with Stephen Douglas, Lincoln delivered his "Apple of Gold" speech on the Courthouse steps, repeating his position that the Constitution does not sanction slavery and, say some, launching his journey to the White House.

Cincinnati

Lincoln's first visit in 1855 was a disaster; the prairie lawyer was snubbed and humiliated by Edwin Stanton, his co-counsel in the McCormick Reaper patent case. Four years later, Lincoln's anti-slavery remarks were pointed, mainly across the river toward Kentucky. His final visit came on his birthday, February 12, 1861. The city's present was a flag-waving, bunting-draped, cannon-booming welcome, where "men grew hoarse with cheering and women wept." The President-elect was "entirely overwhelmed by the magnificence of the reception."

Cleveland

The City Fathers anticipated such a crowd that Cleveland was the only city on the Lincoln funeral train route that opted for outdoor services, hastily erecting a pavilion for the catafalque on Public Square. To save space, ladies were asked to refrain from hoop skirts, and the military escort for the hearse was led by General "Fighting Joe" Hooker, who had lent his name to ladies of less respectable intention.

Columbus

With great appreciation for the many Ohioans who had enlistmented, Lincoln reportedly said that he would like to lie in state in their capitol. The wish was granted. His body lay in the State House Rotunda for 24 hours, during which an estimated 100,000 people came by horse, buggy, and foot to pay their respects.

LINCOLN'S CALL TO ARMS

When the President asked for volunteers, Ohio answered loud and clear, sending to Civil War battlefields, more than 300,000 good soldiers. They were:

- the largest proportion of state population in the North
- in number behind only New York and Pennsylvania
- three of every five Ohio men between 18 and 45
- 5,000 free black troops
- 11,000 killed in battle
- 15,000 who died in hospitals
- 22,000 disabled.

■ *The healing arts and the art of healing as practiced by Ohioans, who, with great inventiveness and dedication, have achieved the admirable distinction of serving mankind and its varied parts*

▶ Daniel Drake learned doctoring from a man in a powdered wig, but Albert Sabin could dispense on a powdery sugar cube a vaccine that stopped the age-old scourge of polio. The difference between them was a hundred fifty years and the advance of American medicine from the near-medieval to the highly technological. This swift and remarkable march was often hurried along by men such as Doctors Drake and Sabin, Ohioans whose discoveries and contributions have helped define the healing arts.

Drake, in fact, began medicine in Ohio. In the early 1800's, his patients were the few hundred souls — not particularly hale or hearty — in the raw river town of Cincinnati. Drake had to battle ignorance as much as disease, and to strengthen the number and knowledge of physicians beyond the Alleghenies, he started the state's first two medical schools. By the time he died in 1852, Drake had trained one-third of the doctors in the Ohio Valley and earned the title of Father of Ohio Medicine.

But more important, Drake spawned in this state an incomparable tradition of men and women serving on the front lines of medicine: physicians such as Crile, who unraveled mysteries that had long bedeviled surgeons; and Cushing, the renowned neurosurgeon; and Favaloro with his heart bypass; and Sabin, the largely unsung polio hero; and on and on. They, like so many members of the extended medical family that Drake began, have proven themselves to be soldiers of mankind's good fortune. Generation after generation, Ohioans have taken up the caduceus in their constant, and often spectacular, fight against death and disease in America.

1800-1849

1805 — First medical diploma west of the Alleghenies issued in Cincinnati to Daniel Drake

■ *Dr. William Goforth thus certifies his apprentice with a scrap of paper that pompously describes Drake as Surgeon-General of the First Division of the Ohio Militia*

1823 — Nation's first teaching hospital in Cincinnati; Dr. Drake's Commercial Hospital and Lunatic Asylum anticipates marriage of academic and clinical medical education by a half century.

1828 — World's first dental college in Bainbridge; Dr. John Harris teaches the specialty in his home

1850-1899

1852 — First woman physician west of the Alleghenies; Myra King Merrick, Cleveland

■ *The lady's homeopathic practice will include John D. Rockefeller, who engages her to attend the birth of his son and namesake*

1869 — "Father of American Neurosurgery," Harvey Cushing, born in Cleveland

" *Dr. Drake is a tall, rectangular, perpendicular sort of body, stiff as a poker, and enunciates his prescriptions much as if he were giving a discourse on the doctrine of election.*"
— *Harriet Beecher Stowe*

Daniel Drake

■ *Cushing becomes world famous brain surgeon and authority on the pituitary gland, discovers adrenal disorder known as Cushing's disease*

1879 — First nurses' training school west of Alleghenies, started in Cleveland

1886 — Nation's first successful appendectomy; Dr. Randolf Hall, a native of Ashtabula County, operates in New York City on seventeen-year old boy

1896 — Nation's first x-ray machine invented by Dayton Miller, Cleveland

■ *After reading about Roentgen's discovery in the* Plain Dealer, *Miller produces nation's first x-ray: the hand of assistant Dudley Wick; also makes first complete set of x-rays of a human body: his own*

1897 — World's first successful amputation under local anesthetic performed in Cleveland

■ *George Crile, gifted surgeon and medical researcher, uses nerve block on seven-year old, who chatters about baseball while his leg is removed below-the-knee*

Nation's first municipal tuberculosis sanitorium in Cincinnati; rural Dunham Hospital isolates contagious victims, provides the "fresh air" cure

1900-1909

1901 — Nation's first medical research center, founded and

funded in New York City by Cleveland's John D. Rockefeller

■ *Rockefeller Institute shores up structure of American medicine with solid foundation of research; breaks new ground in meningitis, polio, yellow fever, syphilis, influenza, heart disease, organ transplants*

1905 — Overexposure to x-rays claims perhaps its earliest victim: the dedicated Dudley Wick, age 28

1906 — World's first successful human blood transfusion performed by Dr. Crile in Cleveland

■ *Other Crile breakthroughs will include developing "shockless" surgery, performing first successful laryngectomy, perfecting thyroid surgery, use of nitrous-oxide as general anesthesia*

Nation's first free dental clinics for schoolchildren started in Cleveland, where Dr. William Ebersole proves that dental hygiene improves health and grades

1910-1919

1917 — Dr. David Marine, Cleveland, announces discovery of a goiter's cause: insufficient iodine; his research has a worldwide effect: use of iodized salt

1919 — First U.S. medical unit dispatched to Europe in World War I; led by Dr. Crile, Lakeside Hospital, Cleveland

■ *Treating battlefield casualties advances Crile's landmark research in preventing surgical shock*

1920-1929

1921 — Cleveland Clinic Foundation started; Dr. Crile gets his own hospital, Cleveland gets a world-class medical center

■ *The clinic's group practice mimics the Mayos, but dedicating chunks of the profit to medical research is, by George, pure Crile*

Nation's first free diagnostic cancer clinic; Ohio State University Health Center, Columbus

1930-1939

1932 — Landmark hypertension discovery; Dr. Harry Goldblatt, Western Reserve University professor, links high blood pressure to reduced blood flow in renal arteries

■ *His experiment probably triggers more research than any other in history, including his own quest to prove that the kidney protein renin causes hypertension*

1933 — First heart tumor successfully removed surgically; operation performed in Cleveland by Cushing disciple, Dr. Claude Beck

1935 — World's first operation for coronary heart disease (angina pectoris), by Dr. Beck, Cleveland

1940-1949

1947 — World's first successful human heart defibrillation, Dr. Beck, Cleveland

1948 — Eureka! in Cleveland; Dr. Charles Rammelkamp discovers that streptococcus bacteria causes rheumatic fever

■ *Rammelkamp spinoff: treating strep throat with penicillin to prevent rheumatic fever*

1950-1959

1952 — Nation's first professorship in cardiovascular surgery; at Western Reserve University for heart surgery pioneer, Dr. Beck

1956 — World's first "bloodless" cardiac surgery

■ *Cleveland Clinic surgeon Donald Effler stops heart beat with drugs, redirects blood flow via chest artery, creates blood-free operating field*

1958 — Rapid human heart and blood vessel movements filmed for first time

■ *Diagnostic breakthrough by F. Mason Sones, Cleveland Clinic; cinematic arteriography lays cornerstone for coronary bypass surgery*

1959 — World's first total aortic and bicuspid valve replacement; performed by Dr. Earl Kay, Cleveland

1960-1969

1961 — U.S. Public Health Service licenses oral polio vaccine; Albert Sabin, Cincinnati Children's Hospital Research Foundation, culminates twenty-five years of polio research

■ *Sabin's superior "live" virus vaccine supersedes Salk's "killed" virus vaccine; Sabin's quest cost $70 million, annually saves U.S. $1 billion in health care costs*

World's first artificial heart; NASA and the Cleveland Clinic develop plastic prototype

■ *Dr. Willem Kolff's artificial organ pumps life into a dog for fourteen hours*

1963 — World's first medical laser laboratory at Cincinnati Children's Hospital Research Foundation

■ *Dr. Leon Goldman, "Father of Laser Surgery," becomes guiding light in surgery and treatment of burns, birthmarks, cancers*

1965 — World Health Organization makes Goldblatt unit the international standard for human renin measurement

1967 — World's first coronary bypass surgery; Dr. Rene G. Favaloro, the Cleveland Clinic, successfully performs the first heart bypass graft using woman patient's saphenous vein

World's first practical kidney dialysis

■ *Drs. Willem Kolff and Yukihiko Nose', the Cleveland Clinic, design blood-cleansing equipment using — appropriately — a washing machine*

1970-1979

1970 — Nation's first residency program, emergency medicine; University of Cincinnati College of Medicine

1974 — World's first surgical cure for Reye's Syndrome; Dr. Robert McLaurin successfully operates on brain of girl at Children's Hospital, Cincinnati

Heimlich Maneuver first described

■ *Cincinnati's Henry Heimlich develops new emergency procedure for choking, a leading cause of accidental death; thus becomes one of nation's foremost savers of lives, some fifteen thousand to date*

1975 — Ohio Nuclear Inc., Solon, produces first commercial CAT scanners

■ *Diagnostic breakthrough scans entire body in three dimensions, photographs soft and hard tissue*

1979 — World's first doctoral program in nursing; Case Western Reserve University, Cleveland

1980's

1980 — World's largest independent cardiovascular treatment center, Cleveland Clinic

1981 — World's first functional gene transfer between mammal species; a genetic engineering milestone for Ohio University, where rabbit genes are successfully produced in mice

Nation's first YAG laser developed by Ohio State opthalmology professor Richard Keates; substitutes shock waves for heat to treat eyes

1986 — World's first test-tube baby borne by a surrogate mother; Dr. Wulf Utian performs in vitro fertilization and implantation at Mount Sinai Medical Center, Cleveland

■ *It's a Girl!*

1987 — Nation's first bifocal lens implant; Dr. Richard Keates, Ohio State University Hospitals, Columbus

Albert Sabin

First Christmas in Ohio — on December 25, 1750, land company scout Christopher Gist read Scriptures to Wyandots near present-day Coshocton, bringing a new Nativity to the Indians, who had been told that Christ was born in France.

First Christmas tree in an American church — at Cleveland's Zion Evangelical Lutheran Church, the Reverend Henry Schwan included a candle-lighted tree in his Christmas Eve 1851 services. Some were offended, but what God and Reverend Schwan joined together, no man has put asunder.

First White House Christmas tree — this Presidential tradition started in 1889, thanks to First Lady Caroline Harrison of Oxford, Ohio. Her holiday cause had an inevitable effect: the entire household — from President to personal staff — staged the first White House tree-trimming party.

Valentine postmark — "There is Nothing in This World as Sweet as Love" is the sentimental slogan of Loveland, the southwest Ohio town whose post office sends those words around the world via a Cupid cachet every February 14. Thousands request the postmark of Loveland, which advances romance by forwarding valentines.

Up On The Housetop — This American classic, a school pageant staple, was written by Benjamin Hanby, who learned music and the ministry at Otterbein College. He wrote the song in New Paris, Ohio, to entertain poor children on Christmas Day, 1864.

Planting Arbor Day trees — although the holiday began in Nebraska, Cincinnati started the tradition in 1882. Schools were dismissed so that children could plant trees dedicated to presidents, authors, and other citizens, establishing the first memorial groves in the U.S.

The date of Thanksgiving Day — when a late Thanksgiving shortened the 1939 Christmas shopping season, Columbus retailer Fred Lazarus, Jr. appealed to President Franklin Roosevelt, who agreed to make Americans forever thankful on the fourth Thursday in November.

White House Easter Egg Roll — Though Lucy Webb Hayes disliked liquor, she loved children. When congressmen complained that egg-rolling was ruining the Capitol lawn in 1878, the Chillicothe-born First Lady invited the unwelcome kiddies to play over at her house.

Labor Day — Senator James Kyle of Cedarville wrote the 1894 bill that established this federal holiday on the September Monday when unions usually held parades; thus the "Father of Labor Day" honored working men and women by giving them a day off.

Oldest Memorial Day parade — Ever since the Grand Army of the Republic planned the first Memorial Day ceremonies in 1868, Ironton has had a parade. Its citizens have so faithfully marched through wars and peace that the town has the nation's oldest such observance.

■ *Nine popularly believed falsehoods, fabrications, rumors, misconceptions, and mislaid facts that have been bandied about with good intentions but poor authority and are hereby laid to a well-deserved rest*

▶ It is said that during the Civil War some politicians came complaining to President Lincoln that General Grant's drinking had gotten entirely out of hand. Lincoln paused a moment, for the General was turning the tide of battle in the Union's favor. Then he replied, "Gentlemen, if I knew what brand of whiskey Grant used, I'd send a barrel of it to every one of my other generals."

Although famous, this anecdote is at best apocryphal. Lincoln himself disavowed the story, though he enjoyed it thoroughly. Most probably, the President's alleged comeback was an updated version of a tale told about King George II, who upon hearing grumblings about General Wolfe's insanity, declared, "Then I wish he would bite all of the others."

The myths presented here are the stuff of such legend, places in the popular culture where truth crosses with tradition. Most are the product of inflation, stories blown up over time until they assume a presence that presumes fact. To these great historical gas bags we give a gentle prick, debunking them respectfully, mindful that they stretch from Shakespeare to Cincinnati and have exhibited enormous staying power, far outliving their original perpetrators. And considering their depth and breadth, we cannot help but agree with H.L. Mencken's conclusion about his unsinkable Cincinnati Bathtub Hoax: "It is out of just such frauds, I believe, that most of the so-called knowledge of humanity flows."

THAT JOHNNY APPLESEED WAS A FRONTIER ST. FRANCIS

Actually, John Chapman was a shrewd Yankee trader who seized the opportunity provided by the pioneer migration into Ohio, planting orchards to fill the swelling demand for fruit and trees. His kindly nature and sincere religious faith fostered the folklore about him, of course, but by the time he died, "Johnny Appleseed" had swapped and sold enough seedlings to accumulate a small real-estate empire.

THAT OLIVER HAZARD PERRY SAID "DON'T GIVE UP THE SHIP!"

True enough, during the Battle of Lake Erie in 1813, the Commodore raised a flag that popularized the phrase, but he apparently borrowed it from a comrade, Captain James Lawrence, who, mortally wounded, had uttered the immortal words three months before. Perry's flagship, by the way, was named *Lawrence,* the vessel where he not only accepted the British surrender, but also gave his own immortal dispatch: "We have met the enemy and they are ours."

THAT CINCINNATI HAD AMERICA'S FIRST BATHTUB

What is probably the nation's most redoubtable hoax was perpetrated by H.L. Mencken. Hoping to lighten the dark days of World War I, he wrote a piece for the New York *Evening Mail* in 1917, which asserted that a Mr. Adam Thompson of Cincinnati had the first bathtub installed in his home in 1842. Much to Mencken's surprise, "A Neglected Anniversary" was taken seriously, and his fictitious mahogany tub with a lead lining was incorporated into history books and encyclopedias. Although his tale about Mr. Thompson inviting the neighbors for a Christmas plunge certainly anticipated today's hot tub, Mencken tried several retractions, but to no avail. His story stuck.

THAT PROCTER & GAMBLE IS IN LEAGUE WITH THE DEVIL

No one seems to know exactly how this ridiculous rumor started, but it was widely bandied about in the early 1980's that the Cincinnati company's famous logo — a man-in-the-moon and thirteen stars — was connected to Satanism. Quite the contrary, the hoary symbol evolved from P&G's pre-Civil War standards of product integrity, particularly the

"For these readers, it appears, all took my idle jocosities with complete seriousness. Some of them . . . asked for further light on this or that phase of the subject. Others actually offered me corroboration! But the worst was yet to come. Pretty soon I began to encounter my preposterous "facts" in the writings of other men . . . They got into learned journals. They were alluded to on the floor of Congress. They crossed the ocean, and were solemnly discussed in England and on the continent. Finally, I began to find them in standard works of reference."

— H.L. Mencken

sterling reputation of its Star candles, and William Procter himself suggested that the logo have a star for each of the original colonies. Even the company's most impeccable product — Ivory soap — derives its name from a passage in the Forty-fifth Psalm. P&G is, of course, the nation's number one soap maker, an irreproachable position as ever was, for as everyone knows, Cleanliness *is* next to Godliness.

THAT CANTON IS THE HOME OF PROFESSIONAL FOOTBALL

While the prototype of today's National Football League was formed in Canton in 1920, the first football games with paid players actually took place a hundred miles to the east in the foothills of Pennsylvania. In 1892, William "Pudge" Heffelfinger accepted $500 from the Allegheny Athletic Association to play in a contest with the Pittsburgh Athletic Club, and in 1895, John Brallier received $10 for his services as quarterback with a YMCA team in Latrobe. The Latrobe eleven bested neighboring Jeannette, 12-0, and Brallier cashed in by becoming the town dentist.

THAT WILLIAM HENRY HARRISON WAS BORN IN A LOG CABIN

The old frontier Indian fighter had actually been born in a mansion, the scion of Virginia's plantation aristocracy, and was living in comparable luxury in North Bend, Ohio, when the Whigs decided that he was presidential timber. The aspersions in a Democratic newspaper about Harrison's log cabin-level ambitions backfired, giving the Whigs a great gimmick for promoting their man, and the modern political campaign was born, complete with rallies, songs, parades, buttons, a catchy slogan — Tippecanoe and Tyler, Too! — and the invented image of the candidate as a common man born in common circumstances. Chances are that Harrison had never even seen the inside of a log cabin, but the Hard Cider Campaign of 1840 made being born in a log cabin — or its humble equivalent — one of the nation's most enduring political traditions.

THAT IT RAINS INSIDE THE AKRON AIRDOCK

In 1928, Goodyear bagged a Navy contract to build the world's biggest zeppelins — the *USS Akron* and *USS Macon* — and the airships required a hanger of comparable proportions. Thus, the tire-maker built the famous Goodyear (now Loral) Airdock, a behemoth in its own right — 1175 feet long, 325 feet wide, 211 feet high, with a volume of 55 million cubic feet. Its sheer size spawned one of Ohio's tallest tales: that clouds form inside the building and cause rain to fall. Some condensation in the airdock's upper reaches? Yes. But actual rainfall? No.

THAT THERE ARE LITTLE GREEN MEN AT WRIGHT-PATTERSON AIR FORCE BASE

In the 1950's and 1960's, Wright-Patterson Air Force Base in Dayton was the headquarters for Project Blue Book, an official military investigation of UFOs that apparently launched stories of bodies of extraterrestrials being stored on the base. The prospect of even a single E.T. on ice in Dayton prompted one man to seek a "writ of habeas corpus extraterrestrial," while another offered the flyboys $3.14 per alien body. In any event, Project Blue Book ended years ago, but the rumors of little green men continue, despite the observer who pointed out that the men at the air base are all clearly *blue*.

THAT THE POPE KEEPS A BEDROOM IN COLUMBUS

Though the Pontifical College Josephinum is the only papally sanctioned seminary in the United States, no Pope has ever slept under its roof. Nor is any Pope likely to, even though folks in Columbus like to think that the sheets are kept constantly fresh just in case His Holiness happens by. In truth, the seminary maintains neither the widely reported bed nor the ever-popular bomb shelter for His Eminence or his convenience.

■ *The causes and crusades of certain single-minded Ohioans, men and women with driving desires, grand plans, ambitious schemes, and convictions firm enough to leave a lasting national impression*

TECUMSEH'S CONFEDERACY

Tecumseh's name meant "Shooting Star," altogether appropriate for a brilliant military and political leader whose heroic life ended all too soon. Born near present-day Springfield, this Shawnee chief tried desperately in the early 1800's to unite the Indian tribes. With white men relentlessly encroaching on the hunting grounds west of the Alleghenies, Tecumseh believed that only by banding together could the Indians preserve their culture and homelands. Pursuing his dream of an Indian confederation, Tecumseh became both warrior and statesman, roles he played with an intelligence, courage, and humanity that even his enemies admired. His constant nemesis was William Henry Harrison, the master land-grabber who secured millions of Indian acres for white settlers. They locked horns at the bargaining table and on the battlefield, and finally, when the War of 1812 gave their frontier tug-of-war international repercussions, at the Battle of the Thames. Both were brigadier generals, Harrison for the Americans, and Tecumseh for his fair-weather British friends. Harrison won, later trading on his Shawnee fight at Tippecanoe to become President. Tecumseh was killed, an incomparable presence — and all hope for an Indian nation — gone at age forty-four.

HOWE'S HISTORIC JOURNEYS

Henry Howe was a thirty-year-old Connecticut Yankee who came to Ohio in 1846 to write a history of the first state carved out of the old Northwest Territory. History, however, does not begin to describe Howe's incredible work, for he spent a year canvassing the entire state on foot and on horseback, catching steamboats and stagecoaches, prowling courthouses and cemeteries, interviewing dignitaries and draftsmen, and all the while filling notebook upon notebook with his observations, information, and drawings. The result was *Historical Collections of Ohio,* a comprehensive treasury of Buckeye folklore, anecdotes, legends, facts, statistics, biography, geography, and, yes, history — political, natural, and social. *Whew.* Howe also did a Virginia collection, but only in Ohio did he perform this editorial feat *twice,* setting off again at age seventy to gather material for an updated edition. "No other State has in its completeness such a work as this," said Howe, "and none under the same extraordinary circumstances of authorship." Fifty years later, the Works Progress Administration embarked on a similar project, sending a small army of writers into every state to chronicle Depression-era America. Not only had Howe shown them how, he had done it alone.

LUCY STONE

Lucy Stone's father would spend none of his money for her college education, which he considered a waste for a woman. So Lucy determined to work her way through Oberlin College in the 1840's. No doubt she found Oberlin's admissions policy appealing, for in 1834, it was the first coeducational college in the United States. The school's liberalism extended only so far, however, for Lucy could not participate in public speaking there, a rather ironic prohibition considering that after graduation she became one of the nation's most sought-after speakers on the lecture circuit. Her forte was womens' rights, particularly suffrage, and in 1870, she started *Woman's Journal,* the long-lived publication of the National Woman Suffrage Association. She also founded the Lucy Stone League, an organization of women who would not adopt their husbands' surnames. Declaring that she would "call no man master," Lucy married Dr. Henry Blackwell of Cincinnati only on the condition that she remain a Stone, which she did until her dying day in 1893.

JOHN BROWN

More than a century after he was hanged, John Brown remains one of the most debated men

"John Brown will make the gallows holy as the cross."
— Ralph Waldo Emerson

in American history. Some consider him a martyred saint, others a certifiable lunatic. On one point, however, all agree: Brown considered the eradication of slavery his divine mission. Brown's character was formed in the Yankee stronghold of northeast Ohio, his family and neighbors being of the staunch abolitionist stock that made the area a prime way station on the Underground Railroad. His failed business ventures in Hudson and Akron were predictable, for Brown believed his true life's work to be freeing all slaves. To that end, he murdered five men, aggravating the bleeding over slavery in Kansas. President Buchanan put a $250 price on his head, and Brown arrogantly countered with a $2.50 bounty on Buchanan. Then in 1859, he and a small band of cronies boldly attacked the federal arsenal at Harper's Ferry, Virginia, in a wild scheme to start a refuge for slaves in the Appalachians. His raid was pitifully inept, but Brown was such a visible lightning rod for the nation's divided passions that Colonel Robert E. Lee and a troop of U.S. Marines were sent to quell the insurrection. At his trial, Brown refused to plead insanity and went to the gallows predicting that only bloodshed would rid the nation of its "peculiar institution." Thus Brown passed into legend, the Civil War proving his final words right as Union soldiers marched to the ditty, "John Brown's Body Lies A'mouldering in the Grave."

THE LIBERATOR OF BULGARIA

When Januarius Aloysius MacGahan was born to Irish immigrants in New Lexington in 1844, certainly no one in Perry County could have imagined that his birthday would become a national holiday in Bulgaria. And it probably wouldn't have if he had found a town job, his failure to do so being the catalyst that took him to Europe, where he learned nine languages and got hired by *The New York Herald* to report on the Franco-Prussian War in 1870. Nationalism was kicking the underpinnings out of Europe's old empires, and correspondent MacGahan followed the armies that settled matters when politics could not. Russia

❝*I am as content to die for God's eternal truth on the scaffold as in any other way.*❞

John Brown

"The correspondents were adventurers-by-proxy, bringing the clatter of hooves and the clash of sabers to breakfast tables where nothing sharper than a butter knife was ever used. With censorship unaccountably lax, with editors blessedly distant, the correspondents were able to write highly opinionated first-person accounts of the events they witnessed. MacGahan became one of the best."

— *Mark Bernstein,* Ohio Magazine

became his surrogate motherland; he was a favorite in Alexander's Court, wed nobility, and could "ride and shoot like a Cossack." When Turkey cruelly squashed freedom fighters in Bulgaria, MacGahan funneled his moral outrage at the atrocities into searing dispatches that both pushed the Czar into rescuing Bulgaria and kept the British from stopping him. His mighty pen had unleashed powerful swords, and MacGahan was acknowledged as "the virtual author of the Russo-Turkish War." He died of typhus in 1878, not yet 34, but the father of the new nation of Bulgaria, which he, with some help from his Russian friends, had liberated.

THE MAN WHO LOVED LIBRARIES

When John Shaw Billings attended Miami University in the 1830's, students could check out only two books a week and only on Saturdays. Billings talked his friends into letting him use their library privilege and thus got *almost* all the books he wanted. Almost, because once when the library was closed, he sneaked in through the roof to spend a few hours of glorious isolation in the stacks. Billings became a physician at the Medical College of Ohio in Cincinnati, and his duties as an Army surgeon took him to Washington, where he collected, organized, and indexed the fifty thousand volumes in the Library of the Surgeon General's Office. It was the first comprehensive medical library in the nation, an enormous accomplishment that made his reputation. In 1896, he became director of the newly organized New York Public Library, where he pioneered everything from building design to branches. Billings's greatest — and largely unknown — contribution, however, was convincing Andrew Carnegie to build libraries. Carnegie directed his philanthropy toward "the improvement of mankind," and Billings's suggestion resulted in nearly 3000 "Free Public Libraries" where English-speaking people all over the world have immeasurably improved themselves. Carnegie spent $60 million, and Billings finally, perhaps, got enough books.

BOECKLING MAKES HIS POINT

In the early decades of the century, when the United States felt newly rich and suddenly brawny and before the Crash brought us back down to earth again, Lake Erie had a pleasure palace where money old and new flowed like champagne. Cedar Point was the grandest resort in America. It boasted the world's largest dance hall, a midway that cost a million dollars, the Great Lakes' largest hotel with water views from *every* room, and a seven-mile causeway that was an engineering and political marvel. Toss in the Venetian lagoon and Tiffany glass rotunda and you get a clear picture of George Boeckling's fantastic Cedar Point vision. He was the Cecil B. DeMille of vacationland, the creator, producer, and director of "The Queen of American Watering Places," and the Queen, in turn, gave him a small empire and a large fortune. When Boeckling died, the Queen declined and nearly died. But in the 1960's, new investors revived Cedar Point, which now amuses America with high-tech wonders such as the Magnum XL-200, the world's highest, fastest roller coaster.

NORMAN THOMAS'S MARATHON

He was born in Marion in 1884, the heir apparent to a lineage of Presbyterian ministers, and he also took up the cloth in 1911, leaving Ohio for a church in East Harlem. When World War I started, Thomas became a pacifist, and profoundly affected by the "grotesque inequalities" and "unnecessary poverty" that he witnessed in New York City, took up Socialism. Though he quit the ministry, he never ceased to be a voice of conscience for the nation, advocating through his prolific pen and ceaseless speeches racial equality, disarmament, and isolationism. A defender of constitutional freedoms, Thomas helped start the organization now known as The American Civil Liberties Union, and from the 1920's through 1950's, he took up where Eugene Debs left off as head of the U.S. Socialist Party. The public knew him best, however, as a perpetual candidate for President and prodded the nation toward a welfare state. Starting in 1928, Thomas ran on the

Norman Thomas

Socialist ticket in six consecutive elections. Even in the discontent of the Depression, he could not pull a million votes, but the dedicated messenger ran again and again, dodging tomatoes and insults, knowing full well that folks recoiled from his Socialist message. Ironically, Thomas was a welcome guest at the White House during the Harding years. Back in Marion where Harding published the newspaper, he had employed Thomas as a newsboy, and the President warmly greeted his old friend as the bright and sincere fellow that he was.

VOLKERT'S COWS
Edward Volkert was lucky enough to be born in Cincinnati, home of the renowned turn-of-the-century painter Frank Duveneck, whose humble subjects and bold, honest style made him a forerunner of the Ash Can school. As a Duveneck disciple, Volkert found a humble subject all his own — cows. In the wake of his failed marriage, cows and oxen became not only Volkert's favorite companions but also a universal presence in his paintings. He had a sincere admiration for cows (whose curiosity he enjoyed) and for their oxen cousins (whose patience made them better posers). The bovines, said Volkert, "have a great individuality," and they became his trademark. From 1903 until his death in 1935, Volkert put a cow in virtually every one of his works, including the triptych mural that still graces the Cincinnati high school where he placed it. His paintings and reputation have appreciated nicely over the years, but a Volkert is not considered a Volkert unless it has a cow.

THE PAPERMAKER
Dard Hunter was the philosophical heir of William Morris's Arts and Crafts movement. His medium was paper, and his message was his unparalleled craftsmanship, which became Hunter's lifelong statement against mass production. In Chillicothe, he learned typesetting at the knee of his newspaper publisher father and dedicated his adult life to the craft of fine printing. His pursuit took him around the world, and Hunter evolved into a master paper-

"I have discovered many curious things about cows. They have a great individuality. I believe they have more curiosity than women. When you go into a field, they come around you to investigate; and if you leave your easel a minute, they will lick all the paint off your canvas."
— Edward Volkert

"Is the sun a little brighter, there in Mariemont? Is the air a little fresher? Is your home a little sweeter? Is your housework somewhat easier? And the children — do you feel safer about them? Are their faces a bit ruddier, are their legs a little sturdier? Do they laugh a lot louder in Mariemont? Then I am content."

— *Mary Emery*

maker of international reputation. In 1923, he became the first man ever to make an entire book by hand. *Old Papermaking* was completely his project. Hunter designed, cut, and set the type, made the paper, wrote the text, printed it manually, bound the pages, and then sold the book himself. Handmade books became his profession and passion, a labor of love that made his small Chillicothe operation one of the most famous presses in the world of printing and publishing.

MARIEMONT
Mary Emery's quiet charity extended from Phoenix to France, and her philanthropy bought hospital beds, and university buildings, and ultimately an entire town. Her husband made a fortune in Cincinnati real estate, and when he followed their sons to the grave in 1906, she found herself quite alone with his money. Unassuming, well-educated, something of a wallflower, Mary was endowed with a sincere sense of *noblesse oblige* that made her a superb practitioner of the Golden Rule. She spent the last third of her life finding useful ways to share her bounty, and in 1923, started her grandest project, Mariemont, a planned community for the working class. Mariemont was her way of providing poor people with a slice of the good life, a green and airy four-hundred-acre suburb of nice homes complete with schools, church, shops, town hall, and village square. When she died in 1927, her will left the money and directive to have her grand plan completed posthumously, and it was. Mary never saw the finished product, of course, which might be just as well, for she did such a beautiful job of fine-tuning Mariemont that it became a haven not for the poor but for Cincinnati's solid middle class.

THE FLAGPOLE SITTER
In the late 1940's, Indians owner Bill Veeck infected Cleveland with a sports fever that probably has never been surpassed in another American city. He was a master showman, a publicity-loving, free-wheeling promoter of major league baseball as well as the Indians.

His gimmicks — from fireworks to babysitters — moved baseball stories from the sports page to the front page and whipped Cleveland into a baseball frenzy in the giddy days when the Indians won the 1948 World Series. Symptomatic of Cleveland's rampant baseball madness was Charles Lupica, who early in the summer of 1949 climbed a flagpole and announced that he would not come down until the Indians were pennant contenders. He stayed there for seventeen weeks, neglecting his delicatessen and missing the birth of his child in a manic exhibit of team loyalty and support. Finally, Veeck had the flagpole dug up, and with Lupica hanging on, it was carried to the stadium, where he finally descended, hailed by the Cleveland faithful like a Roman hero entering the Coliseum. The Indians did not win the pennant that year, and Bill Veeck soon sold the team. But a zany standard had been set: fans of every sports stripe would ever after have Lupica to look up to.

THE STRIKING MR. ABEL
Born the son of a blacksmith in Magnolia, Ohio, I. W. (Iorwith Wilbur) Abel in the 1920's had a "miserable job" in a Canton brickyard. Working for sixteen cents an hour became the burr under the saddle of unionism that he rode his entire life. A millhand during the Depression, Abel once led forty-two wildcat steel strikes in a single year, and in 1942, he helped form the United Steelworkers of America and became its president in 1965. A lifelong member of Canton Local 1123, Abel was a master of collective bargaining, which he practiced with great success during his twelve years as the very popular leader of the steelworkers. His 1973 Experimental Negotiating Agreement with the steel companies was a labor landmark that guaranteed no strikes during contract talks and binding arbitration if words failed. Abel once compared collective bargaining to the art of angling: "You have to have patience and you have to be tolerant. You have to be a fair fisherman. You have to sit back and wait for a bite."

■ *Anarchists, communists, utopians, pacifists, and other dreamers of unconventional American dreams*

THE MORAVIANS

Moravian missionary David Zeisberger started Schoenbrunn and a handful of other villages to bring Christianity to the Delaware Indians along the Tuscarawas River. But even in the wilderness, the pacifist Moravians could not escape war. The American Revolution placed them and their converts in a triple vice: to the west, the British at Fort Detroit; to the east, rebellious Americans at Fort Pitt; and in between, Indian tribes of sharply divided loyalties. The Moravians' earnest attempts to remain neutral only incited hostility and suspicion on all sides and brought tragedy in March of 1782. In one of the blackest incidents in American history, a maverick militia from Pennsylvania methodically murdered the Delaware converts at the Gnadenhutten settlement. Sixty-two adults and thirty-four children were martyred simply for espousing non-violence in a violent time and place.

THE MORMON CHURCH

In 1831, Joseph Smith came to Ohio from New York, where he attracted followers with his claim that the angel Mormon revealed a new religion to him. Though folks in Kirtland balked at his speaking in tongues, the self-styled Prophet there laid the foundation of his Church of Jesus Christ of the Latter Day Saints, commonly known as Mormons. Smith built the first Mormon temple, which was so splendid that the construction was said to be divinely directed, chose the first bishops, increased Mormon membership from about 100 to 4000 in less than a decade, and established several prophet-making enterprises.

THE SHAKERS

Many Utopian sects came to the frontier Ohio after they wore out their welcome in the East, but none would prove more prosperous or ingenious than the Millenium Church of United Believers in the Second Coming of Christ.

The Shakers of Union Village were so often harassed by mobs from nearby Lebanon that in 1820, they felt an Almighty justification to ride through the streets of the offending place and put a curse on it. Not so in Dayton, where folks gave the Shakers and their feverish rites a warmer welcome. The Shakers put their blessing on Dayton, and when word of their benediction spread, many farmers considered it a sign of certain prosperity for the town and moved accordingly. Dayton grew large while Lebanon stayed small, it was said, because of the Shakers.

Commonly called Shakers for the bodily frenzy of their worship, they denounced private property, but advocated hard work, simplicity, herbal medicine, and strict cleanliness. By 1824, the Shakers had six settlements in Ohio, the most successful being Union Village in Warren County, where they introduced animals — Merino sheep, Shorthorn cattle, and their own remarkable hybrid, the Poland China hog — that were an immeasurable boon to agriculture in Ohio and the nation. Ironically the peaceable Shakers were often attacked by mobs, for their communal notions and belief in sexual equality provoked hostility in folks of more conservative persuasions. Within a century, the Shakers disappeared, victims not of violence, but of the most unnatural of causes — their firm belief in celibacy.

"(The Shaker women) were all without exception of a pale and sickly hue. They were disfigured by the ugly costume, which consists of a white starched bonnet."
— *visitor to Union Village, 1840's*

THE MILLERITES
In 1843, a New England man named Miller announced that the end of the world was imminent, and thousands of people prepared to have their bodies taken directly into heaven. In Ohio, the Millerites gave away their worldly goods and, hoping to be nearer their final destination, sought out high places. Cincinnatians waited on hilltops, while Milan Millerites built themselves a tall platform. One fellow even cut off his coattails lest some nonbeliever grab hold and ride them into paradise. When the world failed to end on schedule, Miller announced a mistake in his math and recalculated Armageddon for October 22, 1844. Again, the Ohio Millerites gave away their possessions and took to the hills. Come October 23, they found themselves twice-fooled and considerably poorer in pocket if not in spirit.

THE FREE LOVERS
In the mid-1800's the village of Berlin Heights reluctantly found itself a national mecca for followers of the free love doctrine. The Free Love Society tried several times to start a socialistic community in Berlin Heights. Each one failed, but not before it had attracted "intensely individualized" people who did not mind sharing their spouses along with their

other possessions. The free lovers were fairly successful with their orchards along fruit-friendly Lake Erie, and the villagers objected not to their presence, but only to their "mistaken" ideas. The Free Lovers were prodigious publishers, and editor Frank Barry extended the group's influence by mailing across the country their wonderfully-titled socialist journals — *Good Time Coming, The New Republic, The Optimist, Kingdom of Heaven.* The good women of Berlin Heights, however, were so offended by the liberal perspective of *The Age of Freedom* that they intercepted Barry and the First Amendment at the local post office and made a bonfire of his journals.

THE ANARCHIST

When the United States was changing from a rural to industrial economy in the 1800's, Josiah Warren advocated a "New Society" where people would not need government. Warren believed in the "sovereignty of the individual," which made government not only unnecessary, but also a tyranny. He put his theories to the test in Cincinnati in 1827, where he opened a "Time Store," a highly democratic venture in which customers "bought" goods by bartering their labor. He also published in Cincinnati *The Peaceful Revolutionist*, the short-lived journal that earned him the title, Father of American Anarchism.

THE ZOARITES

An American paradise was lost when the Society of Separatists disbanded in 1898, ending one of the nation's most successful experiments in communism. The Separatists had come to Ohio in 1818, when leader Joseph Bimeler rescued them from the wrath of their fellow Germans, who could not fathom their pacifism or refusal to be baptised. They bought land in Tuscarawas County with borrowed money and called their new home Zoar, after the Biblical place of refuge. Life was so harsh that they resorted to communism and celibacy to survive. Instead of children, they conceived a garden so grand in design and ambitious in scope that it literally and figuratively became their

"It must have been a very pretty village, given the German penchant for neatness. The enormous Zoar garden was tended fastidiously, and the white fences constantly white-washed. 'Scouring and polishing was a daily occupation,' a visitor wrote. 'Floors, benches, pavements, tables, animals and children were scrubbed until they shone. Even the trees were scrubbed.'"

— Sue Gorisek

Tree of Life, their economic salvation. The proximity of the new Ohio Canal was a great stroke of luck, and exporting their splendid produce increased the Zoarites communal worth to a million dollars. Prosperity, of course, allowed them to resume their own reproduction, but apparently on a limited basis. When the Zoarites finally succumbed to the influences of free enterprise and divided their property, they had actually *decreased* in number during their eight decades in Ohio.

THE AMISH

The Amish, whose origins go back to seventeenth century Switzerland, had a peripatetic history in Europe, staying one step ahead of persecutors who took umbrage with their literal Biblical interpretations and belief in adult baptism. In the late 1800's, they arrived in northeast Ohio, put down solid roots, and became eminently successful at agriculture. Though their "modern" discoveries include crop rotation and lime fertilizer, the Amish lifestyle is decidedly and purposefully old-fashioned. They speak "High German" in Church and their peculiar "Dutch" dialect at home. Their religion, virtually unchanged in two centuries, is a strict and unworldly doctrine that manifests itself in their modest clothing and horse-and-wagon farming. Withdrawn from the larger society, the Amish, above all, are a community, and they take care of their own, religiously. In all the world, there are only about 90,000 Amish. They have all but disappeared in Europe, but they built their own peace and admirable prosperity in Ohio, which now has the largest Amish community on earth, some 60,000 strong.

■ *A readers' digest of writers, the novel men and women whose pens and poesy produced a library's worth of fiction, fables, allegories, stories, histories, mysteries, anecdotes and accountings*

Sherwood Anderson — voice crying in the industrial wilderness

Born — Clyde, 1876

Career — at 36, walked out of his position at an Elyria paint factory and into the annals of American literature with short stories that tried to "hear and render the voices of the common people," a people whose reality he saw cruelly violated by the Industrial Age; enormously successful as an *American* writer, his plain, but sensual, style inspired Hemingway and encouraged Faulkner

Must read — *Winesburg*, his classic anthology of small town portraits infuriated most of his hometown but charmed most of America

To wit — "We Ohio men have taken as lovely a land as ever lay outdoors and . . . have, in our towns and cities, put the old stamp of ourselves on it for keeps."
— "Ohio, I'll Say We've Done Well"

Ambrose Bierce — America's first significant writer of black humor

Born — Miegs County, 1842

Career — One of the most proficient literary craftsmen of the nineteenth century, his prose — acerbic and terse — was decidedly modern in tone. Said one critic: "He is not afraid to call a spade a bloody shovel."

Must read — "An Occurrence at Owl Creek Bridge"
The Devil's Dictionary

To wit — "*Edible, adj.* Good to eat, and wholesome to digest, as a worm to a toad, a toad to a snake, a snake to a pig, a pig to a man, and a man to a worm."
— The Devil's Dictionary, *1911*

"For all our professed delight in and capacity for jocosity, we have so far produced but one genuine wit — Ambrose Bierce."
— H.L. Mencken

"As a matter of fact, Anderson is a man of practically no ideas. But he is one of the very best and finest writers in the English language today. God, can he write."
— F. Scott Fitzgerald

Sherwood Anderson

Bromfield liked to point to his barn and say that a check from Twentieth Century Fox had paid the bill. Even his illustrious guests were pressed into service. There's a Mansfield matron who still twitters about the day James Cagney sold her a cantaloupe out by the spring house. The Yankee Doodle Dandy told her that Mr. Bromfield said he had to stay there and work until eight o'clock.

Louis Bromfield — soil-bound sophisticate
> *Born* — Mansfield, 1896
>
> *Career* — wrote Hollywood screen plays and best-selling novels, seven of which were made into films; a world-traveling expatriate, he returned to his ancestral home in Richland County, where he put down roots on a farm, played the country squire to a galaxy of glittering guests, and staked his fortune and literary future in practicing "horse sense" agriculture
>
> *Must read* — *Pleasant Valley, Malabar Farm*, for a sense of his pride in his rural heritage
>
> *To Wit* — *". . . the wealth, welfare, prosperity, and even the future freedom of this nation are based on the soil"* — *Introduction, Pleasant Valley, 1945*

William Riley Burnett — wrote first realistic gangster novel
> *Born* — Springfield, 1899
>
> *Career* — skyrocketed to fame with first novel, *Little Caesar*, 1929
>
> *Must read* — *Little Caesar*, which at the start of the Depression sold 100,000 copies in six months
>
> *To wit* — in 1930, his book was made into a hit movie of the same name, starring Edward G. Robinson and starting the enormously popular "tough guy" movies of the 1930s

Hart Crane — "the greatest voice of his generation"
> *Born* — Garrettsville, 1899
>
> *Career* — a romantic caught in the jazz age, he was the heir to an Ohio candy fortune, although his turbulent personal life was anything but sweet
>
> *Must read* — "The Bridge," the epic poem of 1931, which won a Guggenheim Fellowship for Crane, who invokes everyone from Rip Van Winkle to the Wright Brothers as a backdrop to his ultimate symbol of America, the Brooklyn Bridge

To wit — *"irridescently upborne through
the bright drench and fabric of our
veins"*
— *"The Bridge"*

Paul Laurence Dunbar — *elevated
black dialect into serious verse*
Born — Dayton, 1872
Career — the son of ex-slaves, he was
boosted into a national spotlight
when William Dean Howells gave
him a critical pat on the back; worked
as elevator operator, a sad sign of his
times, but influenced next generation
of black poets
Must read — *Majors and Minors*
To wit — his ambition was "to interpret
my own people through song and
story, and to prove to them that after
all we are more human than African"

Ulysses S. Grant — *in command
of the language*
Born — Point Pleasant, 1822
Career — the Union's Commander-in-
Chief and former U.S. President was
broke and dying of cancer when
Mark Twain offered him $100,000 for
his autobiography; hoping to secure
his wife's future, Grant agreed
Must read — *Personal Memoirs,* a master-
piece of unadorned style critically
acclaimed both as a fine military history and as a watershed of simplicity
in American prose
To wit — *"a man of sterling good-sense as
well as of the firmest resolution"*
— *Matthew Arnold*

Zane Grey — *"Father of the Adult Western"*
Born — Zanesville, 1872
Career — abandoned a career in dentistry
for one in hyperbole, painting stark
contrasts of good and evil, cowboy
and tenderfoot, villains and heroes
that in large part created the Wild
West in the popular imagination; his
own bountiful imagination produced

some ninety books, enough so that even after his death, his publisher printed a new Grey title annually for two decades

Must read — *Riders of the Purple Sage*, his most popular novel

To wit — *"I can never do anything reasonably. I always overdo everything."*
— Zane Grey

Lafcadio Hearn — grandfather of today's "new journalism"

Arrived — Cincinnati, 1870

Career — his detailed, descriptive copy about Cincinnati's back alleys made him a twenty-five-dollar-a-week star reporter whose personal and professional fascination with the unconventional eventually landed him in Japan, where he established a world-wide reputation for his writings on Japan

Must read — "Violent Cremation," *Cincinnati Enquirer,* November 9, 1874, his sensational account of a sensational murder appeared in newspapers nationwide

To wit — *"He prowled about the dark corners of the city, and from gruesome places he dug out charming idyllic stories."*
— Cincinnati Enquirer *editor, John Cockerill*

William Dean Howells — "Dean of American Letters"

Born — Martins Ferry, 1837

Career — editor, *Atlantic Monthly, Harper's, Cosmopolitan;* his prolific pen produced some thirty novels, eleven travel books, innumerable short stories, poems, essays, articles; crony of Henry James, Emerson, Twain, and Hawthorne; son of an itinerant, abolitionist father; child of the passing Ohio frontier; self-educated man who turned down professorships at Yale, Harvard, Johns Hopkins; patriarch of realism in fiction

Must read — *The Rise of Silas Lapham*, a definitive portrait of the self-made man, 1885; *Criticism and Fiction*, in which Howells, the philosophical heir of the egalitarian values of "the West," presents his case for realism and its democratic roots

To wit — *"Real feeling is always vulgar."*
— Letters Home

"Ah! poor Real Life, which I love, can I make others share the delight I find in thy foolish and insipid face?"
— *William Dean Howells,* Their Wedding Journey

Toni Morrison — major protector of postmodern American realism

Born — Lorain, 1931

Career — richly lyric novels about the struggles of black women splendidly woven around the experiences of her kin and the family stories she heard in her Ohio hometown, "where I always start"

Must read — *Beloved*, based on true story of Margaret Garner, a runaway slave who kills her child rather than "be taken back to slavery and be murdered by piece-meal"

To wit — *". . . anybody white could take your whole self for anything that came to mind. Not just work, kill, or maim you, but dirty you. Dirty you so bad you couldn't like yourself anymore"*
— *Beloved*, 1987

William Sydney Porter — created the "O.Henry ending"

Arrived — Ohio Penitentiary, Columbus, 1898

Career — he used a pen name so that his daughter wouldn't find out he was a prisoner in Ohio, but in that confinement, he began writing short stories with an ironic twist at the ending, an innovation in American letters that became his trademark

Must read — "The Gift of the Magi," a Christmas classic: Della sells her lovely hair to buy Jim a watch fob, Jim sells his watch to buy her hair-combs

138

❝ *I hope* Uncle Tom's Cabin *will make enough so that I may have a silk dress.* **❞**

Harriet Beecher Stowe

To wit — "And here I have lamely related to you the uneventful chronicle of two foolish children in a flat who most unwisely sacrificed for each other the greatest treasures of their house . . . Of all who give and receive gifts, they are the wisest. Everywhere they are the wisest. They are the magi."

Harriet Beecher Stowe — the nation's conscience

Arrived — in Cincinnati, 1832

Career — for years, she cast her Calvinist eye on Cincinnati, where the coming Civil War was already being fought on the streetcorners; thus inspired, she penned *Uncle Tom's Cabin*, the juggernaut that crystallized the nation's sentiments on slavery and made her an international celebrity

To wit — "God wrote that book. I merely took his dictation."

James Thurber — an American original disguised as a humorist

Born — Columbus, 1894

Career — went from a *Columbus Dispatch* beat to the rarefied company of *The New Yorker* in a quantum leap of prose and drawings that brilliantly reflected his melancholy vision of love, marriage, and other absurdities of human relationships

Must read — *My World — and Welcome to It*, for his immortal clash of fantasy and reality, "The Secret Life of Walter Mitty"

To wit — "These are strange people that Mr. Thurber has turned loose upon us . . . All of them have the outer semblance of unbaked cookies."
— Dorothy Parker

Artemus Ward — "Father of American Humor"

Arrived — Cleveland, 1857, age 23

Career — writing tongue-in-cheek commentary sprinkled with "horse laugh

It is said that the *Gift of the Magi* was inspired by Porter's wife, Athol. To escape prosecution for embezzlement charges in Texas, Porter fled to Central America, leaving his wife and young daughter behind. As Christmas, 1896, approached, Mrs. Porter was deathly ill, but she summoned the strength to fashion a lace handkerchief, which she sold for money to buy her absent husband presents. When Porter learned how ill she was, he went back to Texas, where he was arrested and convicted. Ironically, perhaps mercifully, his wife died before his trial, and Porter ended up in the Ohio Penitentiary on April 25, 1898, because federal prisons elsewhere were overcrowded.

A purported exchange between Artemus Ward and his mother:
She: "Be good to your mother. Remember what the Bible tells."
He: "I guess I should, but it is so different from The Plain Dealer. *I don't bother with it much. A man can't have two masters, and I'm a Democrat."*

spelling" for *The Plain Dealer* gave this former printer a fictitious identity, which he readily adopted as his own *persona*, setting first Cleveland to laughing and then the entire nation

Must read — *Artemus Ward: His Book,* an anthology of his most popular sketches

To Wit — *"Be sure and vote at leese once in all elecshuns. Buckle on yer Armer and go to the Poles. See to it yer Naber is there . . . This is a privilege we all possess, and it is 1 of the booties of this grate and free land.*
— *"Fourth of July Oration"*

James Wright — blue collar lyricist
Born — Martins Ferry, 1927
Career — world-renowned poet whose intense verses ring with gritty images forged in the mill town of his youth
Must read — *Collected Poems, 1971*
To wit — *"The only tongue I can write in is my Ohioan."*

BEST SELLERS

Uncle Tom's Cabin, Harriet Beecher Stowe — first American novel to get best-seller status; after 1852 serialization in abolitionist *National Era,* sold 2.5 million copies in first year; later translated into 20 languages

Zane Grey — "the world's most popular author" produced some eighty works that generated 139 million sales . . . and counting

Mildred Wirt Benson — in 1930, she penned ***The Secret of the Old Clock,*** the first of many books she ghostwrote for the Nancy Drew series, which sold more than 80 million copies

John Jakes — Daytonian whose series of Kent family chronicles outsold — more than 35 million copies — all other American Bicentennial fiction; in 1978, ***The Bastard*** became the first original paperback ever on *New York Times* best-seller list, and ***The Warriors*** had the largest first paperback printing, 3.5 million copies

The Power of Positive Thinking, Norman Vincent Peale — the good doctor from Bowersville wrote this early self-help book in 1952; 15 million copies sold

Helen Hooven Santmyer — she began her ode to a thinly disguised Xenia, *. . . And Ladies of the Club,* in the 1920s and finished the 1300 page tome in 1982, whereupon her small town virtues — including, of course, tenacity — were rewarded with more than two million sales

General Grant's *Personal Memoirs* — 100,000 sets of this two-volume hit were sold *before* publication, and more than 300,000 after, yielding royalties of some half-million dollars for Grant's survivors

Sex and Racism, Calvin C. Hernton — the Oberlin College sociologist's book has sold more than 200,000 copies since 1966

McGuffey's Eclectic Readers — Cincinnatian William McGuffey delivered his readers in 1836 and in the next hundred years they sold over 122 million copies, becoming the most famous pedagogical tool in America

Emerson Bennett — Cincinnati's crackerjack of the dime novel produced hundreds of short stories, including *Prairie Flower* and *Leni-Leoti,* the 1849 works that each sold 100,000 copies

Dictionary of Marks — Pottery and Porcelain, Ralph and Terry Kovel — the first book by the antique experts from Shaker Heights has had more than thirty-five printings since 1953 ("It has less plot than the telephone book, and it's a bestseller year after year," says Ralph)

"Form a mental picture of a huge burlap bag of potatoes. Then mentally cut the bag, allowing the potatoes to roll out. Think of yourself as the bag. What is more relaxed than an empty burlap bag?"
— *Norman Vincent Peale*

■ John Quincy Adams's last speech — at Wesley Methodist Episcopal Chapel, Cincinnati, 1843

■ Farewell performance of Darke County native Annie Oakley — at Grand American Trapshoot, Vandalia, 1925

■ Last Indian land in Ohio ceded to the United States — twelve square miles surrounding Fort Ferree at Upper Sandusky, by treaty with the Wyandots, March 17, 1842

■ Last President born in log cabin — James Abram Garfield, September 19, 1831, Orange, Ohio

■ Last President with a mustache — Cincinnati's William Howard Taft

■ Last of the Mohicans — settled in Ashland County area in 1700's; immortalized by novelist James Fenimore Cooper, 1826

■ Last riverboat theater still afloat — Cincinnati's *Showboat Majestic*

■ Last runaway returned to the South under Fugitive Slave Law — Sara Lucy Bagby, captured in Cleveland, 1861

■ Sole surviving stern-wheeled towboat in U.S. — Marietta's steam-powered *W.P. Snyder, Jr.*

FAMOUS AND NOT-SO-FAMOUS LAST WORDS

Cleveland poet *Hart Crane* — "Good-bye, everybody!"

President *William McKinley* of Canton — "It's useless, gentlemen. I think we ought to have a prayer."

Wilbur Wright, Dayton — "It was just nerves, I guess."

Point Pleasant native *Ulysses S. Grant* — "Water!"

Industrialist *Mark Hanna,* Cleveland — "But I suppose I cannot have (a handkerchief), my wife takes them all."

Columbus humorist *James Thurber* — "God bless . . . God damn."

Milan native *Thomas Edison* — "It is very beautiful over there."

Oxford, Ohio educator *William Holmes McGuffey* — "Oh, that I might once again more speak to my dear boys."

Dayton lawyer and Copperhead leader *Clement Vallandingham* — "My God, I've shot myself!"

Author *O.Henry,* former guest of the Ohio Penintentiary — "Turn up the lights. I don't want to go home in the dark."

President *Warren G. Harding* of Marion — "What did the (Cincinnati) Reds do?"

Kinsman-born lawyer *Clarence Darrow* — "Let Judge Holly speak at my own funeral. He knows everything there is to know about me, and he has sense enough not to tell it."

BIBLIOGRAPHY

▌

The American Heritage History of Flight. New York: The American
Heritage Publishing Co., Inc., 1962

Andrews, Peter. "How We Got Abraham Lincoln." *American Heritage,*
November, 1988

Baida, Peter. "Breaking the Connection, The story of AT&T from its
origins in Bell's first local call to last year's divestiture. Hail and
good-bye." *American Heritage,* June-July, 1985

Baker, William J. *Jesse Owens: An American Life.* New York: The Free
Press, 1986

Ballantine, Bill. *Wild Tigers and Tame Fleas.* New York: Rinehart &
Company, 1958

Bernstein, Mark. "Mr. MacGahan and the Bulgarian Invasion of New
Lexington." *OHIO* Magazine, November, 1983

Bilstein, Roger E. *Flight in America, 1900-1983.* Baltimore: The John
Hopkins University Press, 1984

Birmingham, Stephen. *The Grande Dames.* New York: Simon & Schuster,
1982

Blue, Frederick J. *Salmon P. Chase: A Life in Politics.* Kent: Kent State
University Press, 1987

Boehm, David A. *The Guinness Sports Record Book, 1987-88.* New York:
Sterling Publishing Co., Inc., 1987

Bogdan, Robert. *Freak Show: Presenting Human Oddities for Amusement
and Profit.* Chicago: University of Chicago Press, 1988

Bordley, James III, M.D. and A. McGehee Harvey, M.D. *Two Centuries
of American Medicine, 1776-1976.* Philadelphia: W.B. Saunders
Company, 1976

Boryczka, Raymond and Lorin Lee Cary. *No Strength Without Union,
An Illustrated History of Ohio Workers, 1903-1980.* Columbus: Ohio
Historical Society, 1982

Brady, John T. *The Heisman: A Symbol of Excellence.* New York:
Atheneum, 1984

Brooks, John. *Telephone: The First Hundred Years.* New York: Harper &
Row, 1976

Brown, Paul with Jack Clary. *PB: The Paul Brown Story.* New York:
Atheneum, 1979

Brown, Sara Lowe. *Rarey, The Horse's Master and Friend.* Columbus: F.J.
Herr Printing Co., 1916

Catton, Bruce. *The Coming Fury.* New York: Doubleday & Company,
Inc., 1961

_____. *A Stillness at Appomattox.* New York: Doubleday &
Company, Inc., 1953

Chandler, Henry Leon. *Henry Flagler.* New York: Macmillan Publishing
Company, 1986

Cincinnati: A Guide to the Queen City and Its Neighbors. American Guide
Series, Writers' Program of the Work Projects Administration in the
State of Ohio. Cincinnati: The Wiesen-hart Press, 1943

Clark, Ronald W. *Edison, the Man Who Made the Future.* New York:
G.P. Putnam's Sons, 1977

Condon, George E. *Cleveland, The Best Kept Secret.* Garden City:
Doubleday & Company, 1967

Connell, Evan S. *Son of the Morning Star, Custer and The Little Big Horn.*
San Francisco: North Point Press, 1984

Conover, Charlotte Reeve. *Dayton, Ohio, An Intimate History.* New York:
Lewis Historical Publishing Company, Inc., 1932

Coxe, Antony Hippisley. *A Seat at the Circus.* Hamden: Archon Books, 1980

Crile, Grace, ed. *George Crile, An Autobiography,* Vols. 1-2. New York: J.B. Lippincott Company, 1947

Crouch, Tom D. *The Giant Leap: A Chronology of Ohio Aerospace Events and Personalities, 1815-1969.* Columbus: The Ohio Historical Society, 1971

Crow, Martha Foote. *Harriet Beecher Stowe.* New York: D. Appleton and Company, 1913

Curran, Bob. *Pro Football's Rag Days.* Englewood Cliffs: Prentice-Hall, Inc., 1969

Current, Richard N., T. Harry Williams, and Frank Freidel. *American History: A Survey.* New York: Alfred A. Knopf, 1979

Cushman, Robert E. and Robert F. Cushman. *Cases in Constitutional Law.* New York: Appleton-Century-Crofts, 1968

Davis, William F. "Ohioan Performs First U.S. Appendectomy." *The Ohio State Medical Journal,* January, 1954

De Bono, Edward. *An Illustrated History of Inventions from the Wheel to the Computer.* New York: Holt, Rinehart and Winston, 1974

De Chambrun, Clara Longworth. *Cincinnati, The Story of The Queen City.* New York: Charles Scribner's Sons, 1939

DeGregorio, William A. *The Complete Book of U.S. Presidents.* New York: W.W. Norton, 1984

Dunlop, Richard. *Doctors of the American Frontier.* Garden City: Doubleday & Company, Inc., 1965

Eberle, Irmengarde. *Modern Medical Discoveries.* New York: Thomas Y. Crowell Company, 1968

Eckert, Allen. *A Time of Terror, The Great Dayton Flood.* Dayton: Landfall Press, Inc., 1965

Ewig, Rick. "Behind the Capitol Scenes: The Letters of John A. Feick." *Annals of Wyoming,* Spring, 1987

Faith, William Robert. *Bob Hope, A Life in Comedy.* New York: G.P. Putnam's Sons, 1982

Fitch, Raymond E., ed. *Breaking with Burr: Harman Blennerhassett's Journal, 1807.* Athens: Ohio University Press, 1988

Fleischman, John. "An Island of Intrigue." *OHIO* Magazine, April, 1983

——————. "Printer's Devils." *OHIO* Magazine, November, 1987

——————. "The Man Who Painted Cows." *OHIO* Magazine, January, 1985

Frank, Sid and Arden Davis Melick. *The Presidents: Tidbits & Trivia.* Maplewood: Hammond Incorporated, 1982

Freidel, Robert and Paul Israel. *Edison's Electric Light.* New Brunswick: Rutgers University Press, 1986

Fried, Albert. *John Brown's Journey: Notes and Reflections on His America and Mine.* New York: Anchor Press/Doubleday, 1978

Garrison, Fielding H. *John Shaw Billings, A Memoir.* New York: G.P. Putnam's Sons, 1915

Gies, Joseph. *Bridges and Men.* Garden City: Doubleday and Company, Inc., 1963

Gish, Lillian. *Dorothy and Lillian Gish.* New York: Charles Scribner's Sons, 1973

——————— with Ann Pinchot. *The Movies, Mr. Griffith, and Me.* Englewood Cliffs: Prentice-Hall, Inc., 1969

Gorisek, Sue. "Ardent Spirits." *OHIO* Magazine, December, 1987

——————. "Of Mice and Medical Men." *OHIO* Magazine, February, 1983

——————. "The Incisive Crile." *OHIO* Magazine, August, 1986

Gunther, John. *Inside U.S.A.* New York: Harper and Brothers, 1947

Hacker, Louis M. *The World of Andrew Carnegie: 1865-1901.* Philadelphia: J.B. Lippincott Company, 1968

Harlow, Alvin. *The Serene Cincinnatians.* New York: E.P. Dutton and Company, Inc., 1950

Harr, John Ensor and Peter J. Johnson. *The Rockefeller Century.* New
York: Scribner's, 1988

Hart, James D., ed. *The Oxford Companion to American Literature.* New
York: Oxford University Press, 1983

Hatcher, Harlan. *The Buckeye Country.* New York: H.C. Kinsey &
Company, Inc., 1940

Havighurst, Walter. *Annie Oakley of the Wild West.* New York: The
Macmillan Company, 1954

——————. *The Heartland: Ohio, Indiana, Illinois.* New York:
Harper & Row, 1969

——————. *Ohio, A Bicentennial History.* New York: W.W. Norton
& Co., 1976

——————. "Primer For A Green World." *American Heritage,*
August, 1957

——————. *The Miami Years: 1809-1969.* New York: G.P. Putnam's
Sons, 1969

Hayes, W. Woodrow. *You Win With People!* Copyright 1973, by
W. Woodrow Hayes

Hays, Elinor Rice. *Morning Star, A Biography of Lucy Stone, 1818-1893.*
New York: Harcourt Brace and World, 1961

Hibben, Paxton. *Henry Ward Beecher: An American Portrait.* New York:
The Press of the Readers Club, 1942

Howard, Fred. *Wilbur and Orville.* New York: Alfred A. Knopf,
1987

Howe, Henry. *Historical Collections of Ohio,* Vol. I and II. Ohio
Centennial Edition: The State of Ohio, 1904

Hubbell, John T. "A Bright, Particular Star. James Birdseye McPherson."
Timeline, August-September, 1988

Hurd-Mead, Kate Campbell, M.D. *Medical Women of America.* New
York: Froben Press, 1933

Hurley, Daniel. *Cincinnati, The Queen City.* Cincinnati: Cincinnati
Historical Society, 1982

Hutton, Paul Andrew. *Phil Sheridan and His Army.* Lincoln: University
of Nebraska Press, 1973

Hyman, Mervin D. and Gordon S. White, Jr. *Big Ten Football: Its Life
and Times, Great Coaches, Players, and Games.* New York: MacMillan
Publishing Co., Inc., 1977

Humphries, J. Anthony. "On an Oberlin Institution of Long Standing."
Oberlin Literary Magazine, May, 1916

Izant, Grace Goulder. *This Is Ohio.* New York: The World Publishing
Company, 1953

——————. *Ohio Scenes and Citizens.* Cleveland: World Publishing
Co., 1964

Jablonski, Edward. *Man With Wings.* New York: Doubleday & Company,
Inc., 1980

Johannesen, Eric. "Stone's Trove: The Legacy of an American Oligarch."
Timeline, June-July, 1989

Johnson, Gerald W. "Dynamic Victoria." *American Heritage,* June, 1956

Kane, Joseph Nathan. *Facts About The Presidents.* New York: The H.H.
Wilson Company, 1981

Ketchum, Richard M. *The World of George Washington.* New York:
American Heritage Publishing Company, Inc., 1974

Klaw, Spencer. "The World's Tallest Building." *American Heritage,*
February, 1977

Klein, Aaron E. *Trial By Fury: The Polio Vaccine Controversy.* New York:
Charles Scribner's Sons, 1972

Kobal, John, ed. *Legends: Clark Gable.* Boston: Little Brown and
Company, 1986

Koenig, Louis W. "The most unpopular man in the north." *American
Heritage,* February, 1964

Laffoon IV, Polk. *Tornado.* New York: Harper & Row, 1975

Laycock, George. *The Kroger Story, A Century of Innovation.* Cincinnati:
The Kroger Co., 1983

Leech, Margaret. *In The Days of McKinley.* New York: Harper & Row, 1959

Lewis, Thomas A. *The Guns of Cedar Creek.* New York: Harper & Row, 1988

Little, Charles E., ed. *Louis Bromfield at Malabar.* Baltimore: The John Hopkins University Press, 1988

Logsdon, Gene. "Pilgrim's Progress." *OHIO* Magazine, August, 1985

Ludlum, David M. *The American Weather Book.* Boston: Houghton Mifflin Company, 1982

Madden, Diane, ed. *Master Builders.* Washington, D.C.: Preservation Press, 1985

Marks, Geoffrey and William K. Beatty. *Epidemics.* New York: Charles Scribner's Sons, 1976

——————. *The Story of Medicine in America.* New York: Charles Scribner's Sons, 1973

Matelski, Marilyn. *The Soap Opera Evolution, America's Enduring Romance with Daytime Drama.* Jefferson: McFarland & Company, Inc., 1988

McCormick, Virginia E. and Robert W. *A.B. Graham, Country Schoolmaster and Extension Pioneer.* Worthington: Cottonwood Publications, 1984

McCullough, David. "The Unexpected Mrs. Stowe." *American Heritage,* August, 1973

McKay, Bob. "Rider of the Purple Prose." *Ohio* Magazine, March, 1988

McMurray, Donald L. *Coxey's Army.* Seattle: University of Washington Press, 1968.

Morgan, H. Wayne. "An Epitaph for Mr. Lincoln." *American Heritage,* February-March, 1987.

Morley, Sheridan. *The Great Stage Stars.* New York: Facts On File Publications, 1986

Morison, Samuel Eliot. *The Oxford History of The American People.* New York: Oxford University Press, 1965

Nicklaus, Jack, with Ken Bowden. *On and Off the Fairway.* New York: Simon and Schuster, 1978

Nelson, Randy. *The Almanac of American Letters.* Los Altos: William Kaufmann, Inc., 1981

Nevins, Allan., *The Emergence of Lincoln.* New York: Scribner's, 1950

Oates, Stephen B. *With Malice Toward None.* New York: Harper & Row, 1977

——————. *To Purge This Land With Blood: A Biography of John Brown.* New York: Harper & Row, 1970

O'Connor, Richard. *Sheridan the Inevitable.* New York: The Bobbs-Merrill Company, Inc., 1953

"Old Clock in Senate Is Alive and Ticking." *New York Times,* December 1, 1983

Ostrander, Stephen. "Penman of Independence: Januarius MacGahan." *Timeline,* June-July, 1987

Peskin, Allan. "The Funeral of the Century." *Lake County Historical Quarterly,* September, 1981

——————. *Garfield.* Kent: The Kent State University Press, 1978

——————. *North into Freedom, Autobiography of John Malvin, Free Negro, 1795-1880.* Kent: Kent State University Press, 1988

Polner, Murray. *Branch Rickey, A Biography.* New York: Athenum, 1982

Pullen, John J. *Comic Relief: The Life and Laughter of Artemus Ward, 1834-1867.* Hamden: Archon Books, 1983

Randall, Emilius O. and Daniel J. Ryan. *History of Ohio: The Rise and Progress of An American State,* Vols. 1-6. New York: The Century History Company, 1912.

Rathet, Mike and Don R. Smith. *Their Deeds and Dogged Faith.* New York: Rutledge Books, 1984

Reichler, Joseph L., ed. *The Baseball Encyclopedia. New York: Macmillan Publishing Company, 1985*

Reston, James Jr. *"You Cannot Refine It." The New Yorker,* January 28, 1985

Rickenbacker, Edward V. *Rickenbacker.* Englewood Cliffs: Prentice-Hall, Inc., 1967

Rickey, Branch with Robert Riger. *The American Diamond, A Documentary History of the Game of Baseball.* New York: Simon and Schuster, 1965

Rodabaugh, James H. "The Cleveland Clinic Disaster." *Museum Echoes,* The Ohio Historical Society, October, 1959
——————. "The Lorain Tornado." *Museum Echoes,* The Ohio Historical Society, June, 1959

Roseboom, Eugene Holloway and Francis Phelps Weisenburger. *A History of Ohio.* New York: Prentice-Hall, Inc., 1934

Rugoff, Milton. *The Beechers: An American Family in the Nineteenth Century.* New York: Harper & Row, 1981

Russell, Charles Edward. *Julia Marlowe: Her Life and Art.* New York: D. Appleton and Company, 1926

Sandburg, Carl. *Abraham Lincoln: The War Years,* Vols. I-IV. New York: Harcourt, Brace, & Company, 1939

Sayers, Isabelle S. *Annie Oakley and Buffalo Bill's Wild West.* New York: Dover Publications, Inc., 1981

Scagnetti, Jack. *The Life and Loves of Gable.* Middle Village: Jonathan David Publishers, Inc., 1976

Schlesinger, Arthur M., Jr., ed. *The Almanac of American History.* New York: G.P. Putnam's Sons, 1983
——————. *The Cycles of American History.* Boston: Houghton Mifflin Company, 1986

Schwantes, Carlos A. *Coxey's Army: An American Odyssey.* Lincoln: University of Nebraska Press, 1985

Sears, Stephen. "The First News Blackout." *American Heritage,* June/July, 1985
——————. *George B. McClellan, The Young Napoleon.* New York: Ticknor & Fields, 1988

Seidel, Frank. *Out of the Midwest.* Cleveland: The World Publishing Company, 1953
——————. *The Ohio Story.* Dayton: Landfall Press, Inc., 1973

Sigerist, Henry E., M.D. *American Medicine.* New York: W.W. Norton & Company, Inc., 1934

Simmons, David A. "Fall From Grace: Amasa Stone and the Ashtabula Bridge Collapse." *Timeline,* June-July, 1989

Smith, Jr., Howard E. *Killer Weather.* New York: Dodd Mead, 1982

Smith, S. Winifred. "The Ashtabula Bridge Disaster." *Museum Echoes,* The Ohio Historical Society, May, 1959
——————. "The Millfield Mine Disaster." *Museum Echoes,* The Ohio Historical Society, August, 1959

Stedman, Raymond William. *The Serials: Suspense and Drama By Installment.* Norman: University of Oklahoma Press, 1977

Steussy, Tod F. "The First Buckeye." *Timeline,* April-May, 1988

Sutton, Ann and Myron. *Nature on the Rampage.* Philadelphia: J.B. Lippincott Company, 1962

Swanberg, W.A. *Norman Thomas: The Last Idealist.* New York: Charles Scribner's Sons, 1976

Toll, Robert C. *Blacking Up: The Minstrel Show in Nineteenth-Century America.* New York: Oxford University Press, 1974

Townsend, Kim. *Sherwood Anderson.* New York: Houghton Mifflin, 1987

Trump, Donald with Tony Schwartz. *Trump: The Art of the Deal.* New York: Random House, 1987

Tucker, Glenn. *Tecumseh, Vision of Glory.* New York: The Bobbs-Merrill Company, Inc., 1956

Utley, Robert M. *Cavalier in Buckskin: George Armstrong Custer and The Western Military Frontier.* Norman: University of Oklahoma Press, 1988

Van Hoose, William H. *Tecumseh, an Indian Moses.* Canton: Daring Books, 1984

150

Van Riper, Frank. *Glenn, The Astronaut Who Would Be President.* New York: Empire Books, 1983

Van Tassel, David D. and John J. Grabowski, eds. *The Encyclopedia of Cleveland History.* Bloomington: Indiana University Press, 1987

Vare, Ethlie Ann and Greg Ptacek. *Mothers of Invention.* New York: William Morrow and Company, Inc., 1988

Vare, Robert. *Buckeye, A Study of Coach Woody Hayes and the Ohio State Football Machine.* New York: Harper's Magazine Press, 1974

Wager, Richard. *Golden Wheels, The Story of the Automobiles Made in Cleveland and Northeastern Ohio, 1892-1932.* Cleveland: The Western Reserve Historical Society and The Cleveland Automobile Club, 1975

Walker, Lois E. and Shelby E. Wickam. *From Huffman Prairie to the Moon, The History of Wright-Patterson Air Force Base.* Wright-Patterson Air Force Base: Office of History, 2750th Air Base Wing, 1987

Wertenbaker, Charles. "Patterson's Marvelous Money Box." *The Saturday Evening Post,* September 19, 1953

West, J. Martin. "Arthur St. Clair." *Timeline,* April-May, 1988

Westerhoff, John H. *McGuffey and His Readers.* Nashville: Abingdon Press, 1978

Weywand, Alexander M. *Football Immortals.* New York: The Macmillan Company, 1962

Wheeler, Lonnie and John Baskin. *The Cincinnati Game.* Wilmington: Orange Frazer Press, 1988

Williams, Trevor I. *The History of Invention.* New York: Facts On File Publications, 1987

Wilson, Edmund. *Patriotic Gore.* New York: Farrar, Straus, and Giroux, 1962

Wittke, Carl, ed. *The History of the State of Ohio,* Vols. 1-6. Columbus: Ohio State Archaeological and Historical Society, 1942

Young, Roz. *Made of Aluminum.* New York: David McKay Company, Inc., 1985

Zinman, David. *Saturday Afternoon At The Bijou.* New Rochelle: Arlington House, 1973